Best Wishes

Ronnie

RONNIE
AND
NANCY

RONNIE
AND
NANCY

A Very Special Love Story

BY BILL ADLER

CROWN PUBLISHERS, INC.
New York

CROWN is a trademark of Crown Publishers, Inc.

Manufactured in the United States of America
Library of Congress Cataloging in Publication Data

Adler, Bill.
  Ronnie and Nancy: a very special love story.

  1. Reagan, Ronald—Family.   2. Reagan, Nancy,
1923-   3. Presidents—United States—Biography.
4. Presidents—United States—Wives—Biography.
I. Title.
E877.A65   1985   973.927'092'2   [B]   85-10946
ISBN 0-517-55845-9

10 9 8 7 6 5 4 3 2 1
First Edition

Contents

The following is an excerpt from President Reagan's radio address on July 20, 1985, after his successful surgery for cancer:

First ladies aren't elected and they don't receive a salary. They've mostly been private persons forced to live public lives. Abigail Adams helped invent America. Dolley Madison helped protect it. Eleanor Roosevelt was F.D.R.'s eyes and ears. Nancy Reagan is my everything.

When I have thought on these days, Nancy, I remember your radiance and your strength, your support, and for taking part in the business of this nation. Thank you, partner. By the way, are you doing anything this evening?

RONNIE
AND
NANCY

1

Rainbow

From the beginning it had been one of those dismal, drizzly, overcast days in late March. The Capitol lay there grudgingly under a leaden gray sky, dirty puddles widening in the pavement between the government buildings. There was no cold or hint of cold in the air—just a soddenness and soggy warmth that permeated the atmosphere, hanging there like an imminent and morbid threat.

On this Monday, the First Lady had an unusually busy schedule, at least for one of the days during her first few months in Washington. At the most, she might have one engagement in a day, but this Monday she had two. However, they were not "public" appearances with the press on hand, just informal receptions—the first at the Phillips Gallery and the second at the home of Michael Ainslie.

The scene from inside the limousine in the White House driveway was not an inspiring one for a longtime resident of California. Leafless branches hung limply in the humid atmosphere. Not a breath of air stirred. The pavement was wet and black.

Anyone would be somewhat daunted by the chilly and sometimes depressing weather of Washington. It took a bit of getting used to; after a few months it did not bother a newcomer quite so much as during the first few days.

Just such an impression may have prompted the President to remark at the close of his first day in the Oval Office:

"It's been a very wonderful day. I guess I can go back to California. Can't I?"

Nancy had always admired her husband's resilience to the twists and turns of fortune. He could disarm the most serious adversary with humor.

Even after listening to his aides, reading the advisories on his desk, and absorbing some of the grim problems of government that first day, he had leaned back and smiled:

"I think I'll demand a recount!"

Whereas an ordinary person might simply have brooded and become keyed up at the thought of what was to be faced, he had taken it all in stride. Even the awesome responsibility of office and the importance of the position had not changed him one iota. He had looked around the residence later and laughed.

"I'm back living above the store again."

His joking reference alluded to his birth in Tampico, Illinois, when the Reagans had lived in a small flat above the store in which his father sold shoes.

Laughter was part of the joy the President and the First Lady shared in their relationship. Ronald Reagan had once said that he joked with Nancy because he loved to hear her laugh. She always was his favorite audience, his best friend, his closest confidante, and his most trusted adviser. Her laughter seemed to enkindle something in him, or possibly it simply reminded him of his love for her.

What amazed her was the rapidity with which those first seventy days in Washington had sped by. It seemed that every minute was filled with some activity or other—activities as diverse as formal receptions and interior-decorating consultations.

Yet at all times, even in the hustle and bustle of the capital city, Nancy had managed to keep her priorities sorted out in her mind. As always, she was determined to keep her family happy. It was a known fact in Washington: if her husband was happy, Nancy was happy. "If Ronald Reagan owned a shoe store," one aide put it, "Nancy would be pushing shoes."

Even before moving into the White House in January, she had determined also to make the residence look its best. After all, she believed that the place where the President of the

United States lived should be "something very special" and a "beautiful, warm place," possessing "dignity and elegance."

Among her outside activities, there were two that she intended to concentrate on especially. The first was the Foster Grandparent Program she had been involved in for several years.

The second was drug abuse among young people, and to attack that problem she had already scheduled a series of meetings at the White House with physicians familiar with it.

Her husband's "eternal optimism"—his attitude that all problems could eventually be worked out—seemed to be affecting everyone around him, including the First Lady!

Barbara Bush, Vice-President George Bush's wife, would be accompanying her to the Phillips Gallery that morning and later to lunch at the Ainslies'. The First Lady and the Second Lady had become good friends in the short time they had been associated with each other. It was, indeed, a far cry from the first days of the 1980 nomination race when George Bush was in the lead, and Ronald Reagan was trying to catch up. The two men had confronted each other time and again—only to join forces at the end to form the redoubtable team that beat Carter and Mondale handily.

Barbara Bush had attended Smith College, from which Nancy herself had graduated. They had not known each other, and Barbara actually had dropped out before her senior year to marry George Bush just after the end of World War II. But the fact that there was such a natural tie in their backgrounds made it much easier for the two of them to get along together.

The Phillips Gallery at 1600 Twenty-first Street was a red brick building with a bay window in the front. Originally the gallery was the home of Duncan and Marjorie Phillips, the couple who had started to build what came to be known as the Phillips Collection back in 1921 during the first year of their marriage.

The collection, composed of nineteenth- and twentieth-century paintings by Bonnard, Braque, Cézanne, Daumier, Goya, Klee, Picasso, and Rothko—as well as Renoir's masterpiece

Luncheon of the Boating Party—became known as one of the best in Washington.

Laughlin Phillips, the son of the original Phillipses, first went into the foreign service and later became a publisher and founded *The Washingtonian* magazine. He took over direction of the collection in 1972.

As soon as Nancy and Barbara entered the gallery, they were gathered in by Laughlin Phillips and his wife, Jennifer. They were taken through the rooms to see at first hand some of the best modern art that could be found anywhere in the country. While they were browsing, Phillips told them some of the stories involving French artists and other notables who had been invited by his parents to dine at the gallery.

Among the many celebrities in the art world as well as other fields who had been guests at the Phillipses' were Matisse, Renoir, Gertrude Stein, Marianne Moore, Braque, Klee, Raoul Dufy, Janet Flanner, André Malraux, Walter Lippmann, Sir Kenneth Clark, and Felix Frankfurter.

Rothko had pronounced the collection his "favorite small museum," according to gallery legend. Bonnard, whose paintings had been popular attractions for years, had encouraged Phillips's mother, Marjorie Acker Phillips, to "draw more"—she was an amateur painter—and she had done so.

After viewing the paintings and chatting with the Phillipses, Nancy and Barbara took their leave, entered the limousine, and began the ride from the gallery to Georgetown, where they were scheduled to attend a luncheon at the home of Michael Ainslie. Ainslie was the president of the National Trust for Historic Preservation.

Fittingly enough, he lived in an old Victorian house at 3021 Q Street, in the heart of Georgetown. Ushered inside the house after leaving the limousine, Nancy and Barbara mingled with other luncheon guests—wives of some of the members of Ronald Reagan's cabinet and other key officials in the White House.

The point of the luncheon was to discuss in an informal way the importance of the preservation of historic monuments in the Washington area, as well as all across the country, and to stress the danger of their destruction to make way for industry and housing—a threat quite evident already and a clear problem for the future.

The discussion was animated, and a number of trenchant ideas were exchanged. Once the meal was over and the talk languished, Nancy announced that she was leaving.

She bade her host goodbye and drove on back to the White House, where she alighted from the limousine at about the time the incessant drizzle of the morning hours was finally calling it quits. Perhaps the District of Columbia might soon begin to resemble California again.

In the first months in Washington, Ronnie and Nancy had spent a good deal of time trying to decide what to do with their Pacific Palisades house—the house that Nancy always considered as "hers" especially. The truth of the matter was that she had never lived in any house of her own until she had married Ronald Reagan. As a small child she had boarded out at her cousin's, and later as a teenager she had lived in a big apartment in Chicago with her mother and stepfather.

She and Ronnie had decided that the Pacific Palisades residence had to go. They could not live in two places at once, and they always had the Rancho del Cielo as a kind of California hideaway to which escape was possible. Besides that, keeping the Secret Service arrangements at Pacific Palisades was costly, especially when that cost was added on to the expense of the security arrangements at the Santa Barbara ranch.

Most of the family furniture had already been shipped East to the White House and was in the hands of Ted Graber, Nancy's interior decorator, who had put together their own living quarters in the White House before they had actually settled in. Now Nancy had Ted working on the refurbishing of the residence—a project that had been started by Jacqueline Kennedy when she was First Lady twenty years before.

The drapes and the carpeting on the third floor were showing signs of wear and tear and needed restoring. The walls needed repainting as well. Nancy and Ted had already visited the warehouse to bring up antiques and furniture from out of the White House's lustrous past to redecorate the place.

Because of media attacks on her "expensive tastes," Nancy had decided that the cost of the interior decorating would be sustained by private donations, and not by the $50,000 budget allocated by the government for the project. It was hoped that the use of private funds would indicate to the press that she was not trying to lay any excessive cost on the nation's taxpayers.

Once in the White House, the First Lady took off her coat and climbed to the third floor, where the painters and carpenters were at work on the extensive renovations that had been planned. She knew that the President was addressing a gathering in town—a union group, as she recalled—and would not be about.

None of the rest of the Reagan family had opted to live in the White House residence quarters—neither younger members nor older ones.

Patti, Nancy's older child, was a particularly stubborn person. She had always reacted negatively to her father's stand against the Berkeley youths while he was Governor of California. She had been against nuclear arms, too. Patti seemed not to want to associate herself with the Establishment even if her father was its key figure—or perhaps it was *because* of that fact.

It was always difficult for anyone to figure out what went on in Patti's mind. She had always been a handful even when she was young, and when she grew up, she took on all the outer trappings of the dissenting youth of the sixties. She had talent. She had acted in television, appearing in roles on series like *Fantasy Island, CHIPS*, and *Love Boat*. Then she had dropped out of Northwestern University after only a short time there and had returned to work in Los Angeles.

What was the most difficult thing to accept was Patti's insistence on living with a guitarist of a rock group. That was the basis of a prolonged difference of opinion between Nancy and her daughter—until Patti had finally left the guitarist and returned to live in the Reagans' Pacific Palisades house. Yet even so, she had proved herself talented enough to write a song that the rock group had sung and recorded.

Nancy's son, Ron, was another problem, in quite a different way. Not a dissenter in Patti's image, he had nevertheless created waves when waves were not needed. Safely enrolled at Yale, he had abruptly announced that he was dropping out of school in 1976 to study ballet. He had moved to the West Coast, studied dance, and then joined the Joffrey II company in New York at Brooklyn College.

Worse than that, Ron had met a young woman in California and had moved into a Greenwich Village apartment with her. Of course, it had all turned out well in the long run. Ron had married the girl two weeks after the election of his father to the presidency. True to form, he had avoided a big family wedding and had married her in a civil ceremony in New York—*telephoning* his mother with the news. Wasn't that just like a product of the sixties?

Yet his debut at the Metropolitan Opera House at Lincoln Center just two weeks earlier had been an equally important event in the life of a show-business person. And Nancy and Ronnie had been there to savor it.

There was always Michael, who had been married twice and who always seemed to distance himself from the family—at least in a physical sense. Yet he was unusually ready to talk to the press. And he was father of the President's only grandchild—Cameron Michael Reagan.

It was Maureen whose activities were creating shock waves again. Twice divorced, she was being married again in May. Yet Maureen had been a solid rock during the campaign, working as hard as anyone else—perhaps even harder—for her father's election.

If only Maureen . . .

Nancy was standing in front of an elevator in the guest quarters of the White House residence when she became aware that a Secret Service operative was trying to attract her attention. He was holding a walkie-talkie in his hand, and his face was expressionless but somehow tense. Something must be wrong. It was not usual for the security people to interrupt anyone in the residential area.

"Mrs. Reagan," the agent said softly, "there's been a shooting at the hotel."

Shooting? What hotel? Of course. The President was speaking at the Washington Hilton.

"The Hilton?"

"Yes. Your husband was not shot. They tell me he was not hurt."

"Where is he?"

"At the hospital. He's been driven to the hospital, they say."

"Of course. We'll drive there immediately," she told him. She went for her coat.

The agent demurred. "A number of people who were with the President have been shot. We believe you should wait here for now."

"We'll go," Nancy said stubbornly.

"We don't think it's the best place for you to be."

"I'll decide that," she said.

Upon closer questioning, it became evident that the agent had been in conversation with one of the President's aides calling from the hotel. It was the opinion of both the aide and the agent that the First Lady should stay away from the hospital.

"Nonsense," she told him. "I'm going over. Where is he?"

Reluctantly the Secret Service operative told her that the President had been taken to George Washington University Hospital, located about a mile and a half from the White House. Nancy immediately ordered her limousine to pick her up and take her to George Washington Hospital and then rushed downstairs.

Within minutes she was in the backseat and the limo was moving out into traffic. She had always been a worrier, and something like this—even though Ronnie was not involved in it—brought on all kinds of pangs and emotional pressures. What if he *had* been involved? Her mind raced on. What would she do then?

Jack Benny had once told her what it meant to him to be a worrier.

"I'm a worrier," Jack had said. "You're a worrier. Doesn't it annoy you when people say to you, 'Nancy, you've got to stop worrying'? They just don't realize that you're born a worrier, and you'll die a worrier!" Jack was right.

But this time, at least, Ronnie was *not* hurt.

Threats on Ronnie's life were not new. Nancy remembered one night in 1968 back in Sacramento. That was a very bad year. Martin Luther King and then Robert F. Kennedy had been killed. Even in Sacramento, security had been tightened.

In the Governor's Mansion, Nancy and Ronnie were awakened in the middle of the night by a sound that Ronnie immediately identified as a gunshot. Nancy remembered watching in terror as he got up, put on his robe, and went out into the hall. There he was confronted by a Secret Service man walking down the corridor carrying a shotgun.

"Governor," the agent said politely, "would you mind not getting in front of any windows?"

And with that warning firmly implanted in his mind, Ronnie had come back to bed.

Later they discovered that one of the agents had seen two men trying to ignite a Molotov cocktail beneath the windows where Nancy and Ronnie were sleeping. The agent had fired one shot, but did not dare to fire again at the two men running to their getaway car.

However, the unlighted firebomb was there in the morning. Nancy had been profoundly disturbed to see that their firebomb was a magnum-sized champagne bottle, not just a soft-drink bottle as she had automatically supposed. What a fire that would have made, flung through the window and onto the bed!

Nancy tried to shake off the memory, but another intruded. This had been a more specific threat—one directed against Nancy and not Ronnie. An undercover agent had unearthed a plot to kidnap Nancy and send her head to Ronnie if he wouldn't agree to release some people from a California prison!

Nancy's habit of worrying always forced her mind into strange channels. Now even in the admittedly false security of the limousine's interior, it was difficult to dwell on danger and peril. The public had always been nice to the two of them during the campaign, even with political opponents in evidence. She and Ronnie had discussed the outpouring of affection and warmth from the crowds who pressed in to meet them. She had never felt any fear of attack during those encounters with the public.

And yet, of course, all people who occupied sensitive positions in any country's power structure were always subject to terrorist attacks and other overt forms of hostility. That was a fact of modern life.

The limousine turned into the driveway of the hospital and slammed to a stop. Nancy fumbled for the door handle to get out. She did not know it, but she had arrived only minutes after the President had. She had to find him, had to talk to him, had to find out who had been hurt, had to find out what it was all about.

As she came out of the limousine, she saw Michael K. Deaver, one of the President's chief aides, standing at the door of the hospital, obviously waiting for her. It was apparent that he had been alerted by the Secret Service to the fact that she was on her way.

Deaver had joined the Reagans when Ronnie had run for Governor of California and had remained with him ever since, out of service for only a brief interval. He handled Ronald Reagan's public relations—making sure that what was printed about him was true and represented him as he should be portrayed and as he wanted to be portrayed.

His ancillary duties included watching over Nancy and making sure that she was aware of what her husband and his aides were doing so that there would be no slipups or errors caused by lack of communication.

Nancy liked Deaver particularly. His wife, Carolyn, was a kindred soul; she too had gone to Smith College, but quite a few years later.

She now found herself running toward Deaver. She seemed to be babbling something out as she quickly crossed the pavement toward him.

"He's all right," she was crying out, perhaps in an unconscious effort to prompt Deaver into agreeing. "He's all right," she called out again.

Deaver watched her closely. "He's taken a bullet," he said slowly, waiting for the effect of the words to sink in and make sense to her.

The First Lady said nothing. She was close to Deaver now, looking up into his eyes with those enormous, clear, wide hazel eyes of hers. She seemed to think about what he said.

"He's wounded," Deaver went on when he saw that she did comprehend what he had said and was not in any danger of going to pieces. "But only slightly."

So there had been a shooting. Ronald Reagan, the President, had been hit with a bullet. He was still alive. There were others hurt, but it was he whom she wanted to see. There was only one thing to do, only one thing to say, and she said it: "I want to see him."

Deaver nodded and moved off. Now Nancy had to be aware of the bedlam all about her. People were running around in all directions, orders were being shouted from place to place, all seemingly without coherence.

And yet at the same time, there seemed to be a concerted and even studied effort to mount an important life-saving operation within the confines of the hospital walls.

"I want to see him," she said again, this time to a man whom she did not recognize but who was standing next to her. "I want to go to him."

Almost at the same instant Michael Deaver returned from wherever he had gone. He told her that the President was in an emergency room down the hall.

"I want to go to him," Nancy repeated.

Deaver nodded. "Yes. But you'll have to wait a bit."

He was stalling. What was the matter? "Why can't I see him if he's all right?" she asked. Nancy Reagan was not a person who panicked easily; not a person whose nerves shredded away at the slightest crisis. They said she had nerves of iron, even though she was a chronic worrier.

A stranger hurried up to Deaver and nodded his head silently, and then Deaver took Nancy's arm in his.

"Come," he instructed her.

They moved carefully down the bustling corridor to a room at the end of it, Bay 5A. Nancy's, father, Dr. Loyal Davis, was a neurosurgeon, and she had trained as a nurse's aide at one time. She guessed that Bay 5A was an emergency room where patients were first taken for examination. In the end her guess proved to be right.

As she entered Bay 5A through the door, she could see him there on a mobile table—the President, Ronald Reagan, Nancy's husband of twenty-eight years. She was struck immediately by the paleness of his face. He had lost an incredible amount of blood and seemed to be extremely weak. But he saw her, and by his look it was obvious that he was able to communicate with her.

She leaned over to kiss him, and as she touched him he lifted the oxygen mask that covered his face and said in a very hoarse voice: "Honey, I forgot to duck!"

Nancy straightened up and reached out to grip his hand. She said something at once reassuring and probably not terribly original, something that was lost in all the excitement and turmoil about them. A look of astonishing pain and surprise crossed his face. The President seemed momentarily unable to breathe. He tried to speak, but there were no words.

He shook his head slightly, but no sound—no breath—came. One of the attendants quickly adjusted the oxygen mask and glanced warningly at her.

Nancy understood, but now she was frightened—terribly frightened. Somehow she managed a smile, and was gratified to see that he was able to see it and smile at her in turn.

Their moment together did not last long. In a moment they wheeled him out toward what she knew must be the operating room.

Deaver was at her side and took her down the corridor, where she was handed over to one of the officials of the hospital, who led her to a very small room away from the sounds of scurrying and excitement. It was windowless and painted a bilious green. It contained a folding cot used by doctors on duty during the night shift and a pile of empty crates and boxes stacked against one of the sickly walls.

She hated the room. It was a room that could absorb hate. Wondering what to do, she sat there with several of the Secret Service agents and others. She tried to clear her mind of all the conflicting and random thoughts that were rushing through it. She could feel the unreality of the room. Its very remoteness and its tininess made it seem like something out of a mad *Alice in Wonderland* dream.

She knew that she must manage to get hold of herself, or else she would come apart completely, unraveling like a much-loved doll whose stuffing had come loose. If she was unable to keep her own presence of mind, someone would have to be responsible for her, and that would make it all the more difficult for the hospital staff to cope with the President's wounds and the wounds of the others who had been hurt.

Then she was not alone. Ed Meese and James Baker, two of the President's so-called troika—the three top aides to the Chief Executive—joined her. Meese carried the title of "counselor"; Baker was "chief of staff." The third, of course, was Deaver, whose title was "deputy chief of staff."

She learned to her horror that James Brady, Ronnie's press secretary, had been badly wounded, along with a Secret Service agent and a Washington policeman. She learned that the would-be assassin had been captured, but did not find out anything else about him.

The word "Rawhide" filtered in to her from the corridor. That was Ronnie's code name; hers was "Rainbow." What an irony! Rainbow. Colors bright and cheery in this little agony of a room done in sick green.

She was frightened, and she had to admit it. For some reason, she had not bothered yet to ask anyone exactly where the bullet had hit her husband. It was the terrible agony in his eyes when he had tried to breathe and had been unable to that had unnerved her. If he had trouble breathing, perhaps he had been shot in the chest. . . .

It did absolutely no good to let her mind wander untethered and imagine all sorts of dire things. Courage, she cautioned herself. Courage.

After the President's aides had talked to her and gone, she managed to get out of the cramped room and discovered a small chapel somewhere in the bowels of the hospital. She stayed in there, for it was quiet and safely away from where Ronnie was being ministered to.

It was second nature to her to say a prayer to call up strength from the wellsprings of her faith, strength that would help her revive herself. And there, silently and cleansingly, she wept a little.

2

Rawhide

For the President, the day had begun promisingly enough, although certainly the weather was not at its best. But then, the weather never seemed to be at its best in Washington. Far away in California, the weather probably *was* wonderful, as usual.

Ronald Reagan had begun his day with a meeting of 140 officials on a subcabinet level in the East Room of the White House. There, to their enthusiastic applause, he had delivered a short pep talk, much in the manner of the institutional pep talks he had delivered years before to business executives he had been hired to inspire with corporate enthusiasm.

The main point of his talk was the need for change in the country's economic policy. He ended the speech with a quotation from Tom Paine that he often found useful: "We have it in our power to begin the world over again."

After that he held a short meeting with members of the senior staff at the Oval Office. With all of his most important aides, he outlined the agenda of the day and for the immediate future.

He then spoke to two dozen Hispanic leaders in the cabinet room, after which he posed for press photographers with Lyn Nofziger and Elizabeth Dole, two important Administration aides.

Normally, the President and the First Lady would have been eating lunch together, but today Ronald Reagan settled down alone to a meal of avocado, chicken salad, sliced red beets, and an apple tart. It was typical of the rather sparse fare at the

White House since the Reagans had taken up residence there. It was also typical of their fondness for fresh vegetables and fruits and for lean foods.

After lunch he worked briefly on the speech he would deliver in the afternoon at the Washington Hilton to 3,500 members of the building and construction trades department of the AFL-CIO. It was to be the largest group the President had addressed since assuming his role in the Oval Office.

For the affair, he dressed carefully in a blue pinstripe suit—brand-new—with a white monogrammed shirt, making sure that the white handkerchief stuck out of his dress pocket in the approved manner he had learned long ago in Hollywood.

Although he was a union man himself and had, in fact, been president for a number of years of the Screen Actors Guild, one of the most active unions in the entertainment industry, he knew that the men waiting for him in the ballroom of the Hilton were not exactly his greatest admirers. In fact, none of these unions had supported him in the recent election. In addition to that, he knew that there had been over half a million construction workers out of work at the time he had taken office; he also knew that they were not yet back on the job.

Nevertheless, as he entered the Hilton International Ballroom that afternoon, where the union members were waiting, he received a standing ovation. But there all adulation seemed to end. As he proceeded to deliver what he had considered to be a surefire speech, he could see that he was not exactly enthralling this audience of union members. Even though he tried to snap up his delivery, giving stress to certain words in a time-tested fashion that usually got him a good response, he realized that he was not coming through to them as well as he felt he should be able to.

Although his delivery was a bit flat, he was interrupted four times with applause during the execution of the speech. This gave him hope that he might be able to win over at least *some* of his union associates and confreres to the Republican side sometime in the near future.

At one point in his speech he made the following statement:

"Violent crime surged ten percent, making neighborhood streets unsafe and families fearful in their homes."

This statement would be picked up later; it dramatically foreshadowed the macabre act that was to come.

At 2:24 P.M., the speech over, the President and his retinue began their departure from the Hilton ballroom for the seven-minute drive back to the White House. The Hilton International in Washington is equipped with a special VIP entrance-exit on the side of the building. With double doors of steel, protected by an overhanging concrete canopy, it opens out onto a sidewalk thirteen feet wide running along a curving driveway. A retaining wall fifteen feet high, made of ornate stone, follows the driveway.

In addition to providing ease of access, the exit was designed to allow celebrities of one kind or another to enter and leave the premises with some degree of safety from overenthusiastic well-wishers, friends, or fans. The Secret Service White House detail had roped off an area twenty-five feet from the door to keep onlookers at a distance during the President's departure.

Coming briskly along the thousand-yard-long carpeted corridor to the double doors, the President stepped out onto the sidewalk leading from the exit to the driveway, where the White House limousine waited at the curb, its motor running. He was aware almost immediately that the dismal Washington drizzle had finally abated. The day was looking better already. The air, although soggy, was warming up.

He strode toward the limo, which was parked about fifteen feet from the VIP exit and about ten feet from the rope that was holding off the curious onlookers. Behind the rope stood members of what the press calls the "body watch."

This "watch" was a group of television and still photographers, along with a handful of ambitious reporters and stringers, who made it their business to wait around for VIPs on the chance that a celebrity might make an off-the-cuff remark in response to a random question from the crowd. Most members of the body watch were off-duty or free-lance photographers and writers.

The press knew the President's tendency to answer an informally posed question. For that reason, he always attracted a large number of hopeful body watchers before and after every public appearance known to the press in advance.

As Ronald Reagan walked toward the limousine, he was accompanied not only by the Secret Service agents who made up the White House detail in charge of his security but also by several of his top White House aides. On his left, between the roped-off body watch and himself, was Mike Deaver. Although Deaver did not always come with the President to such occasions, he had decided to do so today.

Just behind Deaver came the President's press secretary, James Brady. Although Deaver was Brady's boss and had some say in the handling of the press, he had never served as press secretary himself, nor did he indulge in the general give-and-take that a press secretary shares with members of the press.

Waiting for the President at the limousine was Secret Service agent Timothy J. McCarthy. Nearby stood Secret Service agent Jerry S. Parr and a Washington policeman named Thomas K. Delahanty. Seated in the driver's seat of the presidential limousine was Secret Service agent Drew Unrue. All these were familiar faces to the President, who from his Sacramento days was accustomed to the crowd of people who always followed him wherever he went in public.

As the President stepped briskly along the sidewalk, he waved jovially to the members of the press behind the rope. Seizing what might prove to be an opportunity for an off-the-cuff remark, Michael Putzel, of the Associated Press, called out a question about current developments in Poland, which seemed to be approaching the crisis stage.

The President heard the question and began to form an answer, but James Brady pushed ahead, waved the President aside, and approached the rope to give Putzel some kind of prepared answer. Deaver, who was walking ahead of Brady, moved aside and headed for a second limousine, called the "control car," that usually followed the presidential limousine.

He would share that limo with David Fischer, a young lawyer and a protégé of Deaver's, now serving as a presidential aide-de-camp.

At that moment, just as Brady strode toward the roped-off group making up the body watch, the entourage was startled by the sound of two rapidly fired gunshots. Although they were not particularly loud and in fact sounded a bit like small firecrackers, the Secret Service agents immediately sensed that the threat could be very real and very dangerous. After a split second, four more shots followed, in rapidly fired sequence—with immediate and devastating results evident in the street and on the sidewalk.

James Brady, in front of the President, fell heavily to the sidewalk. Timothy McCarthy, who at the sound of the first shot had turned toward the group at the ropes, fell back and slumped to the ground, hit in the abdomen. Thomas K. Delahanty, the Washington patrolman, fell to the sidewalk and began screaming in pain at the bullet that had lodged in his neck.

Deaver later reported what he had seen and heard at the crucial moment:

"When you're in a very tense [crowd] situation, you think about it and you're very alert, looking at people. There was no reason to think about trouble that day. I hadn't taken but a couple of steps when the first shot came over my right shoulder. It was close enough for me to feel the concussion and smell powder. There was no question in my mind. I mean I went *down* because I *knew*.

"The shots just kept coming and I crouched behind the trunk of the limousine until I could see that the President was in. I was thinking, My God, it's happening. After all those times when you think about it, it's actually *happening*. Those shots kept coming. I saw people going down, not realizing [myself that] they were hit. I thought they were just protecting themselves."

Deaver did not identify the gun or the gunman. Neither did the President.

"I never saw the man with the gun," Ronald Reagan recalled later. "I didn't even know I had been shot."

However, he did intuitively understand what had happened. He saw Deaver to his left duck down and move away from him. There was no need for him to plan any kind of reaction at all. Behind him Secret Service agent Jerry Parr immediately jumped on him, pushed his head down, and shoved him forward powerfully, through the open door of the car. The movement was so quick and so forceful that the President hit the top of his head on the roof of the doorway. Then he felt himself falling forward with the Secret Service man weighing him down heavily.

The two men huddled on the rounded transmission hump in the center of the limousine. The President lay on the bottom, his body sheltered by Parr's. Somehow, in that awkward position, Parr got the door closed and called out to the driver, who was staring out at the sidewalk in a stunned and benumbed astonishment.

"Take off!" Parr cried.

When there was no immediate response on the part of the driver, he called out again:

"Just take off!"

Now the limo roared into belated motion and screeched down the driveway, burning rubber in a television-type getaway, screaming out into the busy Washington traffic.

Lying on the floor of the limousine, the President could feel a shattering pain in his chest.

"Jerry, get off me," he ordered the Secret Service operative. "You're hurting my ribs. You really came down hard on top of me!"

The President believed that the agent had forced him through the open door and into the car with such haste and energy that he had broken one of his ribs when he had hit the driveshaft housing.

The limousine was now careening rapidly along the crowded streets of the capital. The two men struggled to a sitting position in the back of the spacious limousine.

The driver turned his head. "Where to?" he asked Parr, who was head of the White House detail in charge of the President's safety.

Parr had an answer ready. "The White House."

Quickly Parr turned to the President and began to explore his chest, under his arms, and ran his hands over his back, observing him at the same time with anxious eyes. There seemed to be no wound evident.

On his part, Ronald Reagan was numbed with shock and enveloped in waves of pain and nausea as he sat there, submitting to Parr's explorations.

Parr now got on the walkie-talkie to the White House Secret Sevice command post.

"Shots fired," he said. "Rawhide returning to Crown." "Rawhide" was the President's code name, "Crown" the code name for the White House.

Turning once more to observe the President, this time with a bit of diffidence, Parr went on speaking into the walkie-talkie: "Rawhide not hurt. Repeat. Not hurt."

The limousine sped through the tunnel under DuPont Circle, a few blocks away from the Hilton. The President was still concerned and puzzled about the enormous pain he could feel in his chest. He might have been hammered in the ribs. Now he complained to Parr that he was even having trouble breathing. At his side, Parr was now gazing at him in some alarm.

Parr could see the President's face, whereas the President could not. He could see that Ronald Reagan, who usually had a high-colored flesh tone, was turning a pale, glazed, ashen shade of white. He definitely seemed to be having trouble getting in fresh air.

Suddenly the President began to cough and had a great deal of trouble catching his breath. Then in horror Ronald Reagan felt something warm dribbling down his chin. He could not see what it was.

Parr could see—plainly. It was blood. It was very red, very bright red: oxygenated blood coming directly from the lungs. Instantly Parr knew that the President's lungs might have been penetrated in some fashion—possibly by the "broken rib" he had been hinting at.

"I felt very badly," the President recalled later, "and then I was bleeding through the mouth. It first came to my mind, with the paralyzing pain as I landed in the car, that I'd broken a rib [when Parr pushed me into the backseat]. And then when the blood started to come out of my mouth, I thought, The rib is broken and it punctured a lung."

Immediately Parr was on the radio calling the command post at the White House.

"Rawhide is heading for George Washington."

Parr leaned forward and talked directly to Unrue in the front seat.

"Head for George Washington Hospital," he told the driver in a low voice. "We've got a problem."

Unrue nodded and corrected his route at the next corner so that they would soon be arriving at George Washington Hospital, which was located a mile and a half from the Hilton and about the same distance west of the White House.

The President heard the words and turned to Parr almost lethargically. "Why are you changing direction?"

Parr answered him quickly: "We're just going to check you out at GW."

That made sense. If his rib was broken, and his lung injured, he should be examined by doctors. He sank back in the comfortable upholstery and tried to stifle the welling lethargy that seemed to be taking over.

Then Parr was on the walkie-talkie again, this time to the White House command post. "Notify the hospital that Rawhide is en route."

The President closed his eyes. In moments, it seemed, they were cruising up the driveway to the emergency entrance of George Washington. The President could feel his strength ebbing, but he determined not to let it show. He pushed away Parr's hand when he offered to help him out of the car. Parr backed away, seeming to understand that the President wanted to walk unaided to the hospital.

22

Parr climbed out and held the door open. Almost by will-power alone Ronald Reagan managed to exit the limousine while everyone stood around looking at him, shocked by the pallor of his face and the shadow of pain in his eyes.

At this moment the control car carrying Deaver and Fischer slammed up behind the limo that had brought the President. Deaver hopped out, followed by Fischer. They stood there watching in stunned dismay as the President slowly and pain-fully willed himself out of the car and into the hospital.

Parr stood beside the President, watching anxiously, as he moved toward the emergency entrance and almost staggered as he entered the corridor beyond the doors.

"I feel as if I can hardly breathe," the President gasped.

Deaver later made a formal statement of those moments:

"The President got out on his own and started to walk in with the help of agent Jerry Parr. We got inside the doors and through the waiting room and just at the end of the waiting room going into the emergency room the President went down—slowly—and he was picked up by three or four people and they started ripping his clothes off and carrying him at the same time, and he seemed to be in a lot of pain. He was gri-macing, and there was a lot of confusion, obviously, at that point—aides, doctors, nurses, Secret Service agents."

As the President's eyes rolled upward and his knees started to buckle, a nurse grabbed his arm, and two paramedics as-sisted her in holding him upright as they half-carried him down the forty-foot corridor to Bay 5A, the hospital's "trauma" bay, or emergency room.

There he was helped up onto one of the beds. He lay there flat, with the bright lights of the room shining in his eyes. He was frowning in his discomfort, obviously hurting. As he lay there he looked about him almost unseeingly. He muttered something that no one could make out, and then finally, fight-ing to get air into his chest, he whispered: "I feel so bad."

The room was crowded now. Secret Service agents were there, the Washington police, doctors, technicians. It was bed-lam. The President himself was in a fog of pain—what physicians technically regard as "trauma." He was being poked at and prodded by dozens of fingers and instruments. As he lay there, the President realized that he had lost all control over his energy and his strength. It was simply drifting away from him, and he could do nothing about it.

At the head of the bed he was conscious that Parr stood, waiting. At the foot of the bed there was a man who seemed to be a doctor, although it was hard to tell in such a crowded room.

The doctors and nurses were cutting his brand-new pinstripe suit from his body. He was conscious of it, but he did nothing to protest. Later he recalled:

"I knew from the manner in which I was unclothed that I probably wouldn't wear that suit again."

The doctors and nurses could see a great deal more than the President had seen and than Parr had been able to see—there was a bloody wound that had been made by the entrance of a bullet or bullet fragment.

All the President could hear was the murmur of low voices, expressing medical details in the flat tones of operating-room jargon, deliberately couched in terms that a layman could not understand.

Although he was not aware of exactly what words he had heard—if indeed he had heard any—the President was now aware that he had been shot at and had been hit.

They brought up an oxygen mask and slipped it over his nose and mouth. An intravenous tube was strapped to his arm, and he was beginning to receive blood. One doctor gave him a shot of anesthetic in the side. Then the doctors got to work.

They made an incision in his body and put a tube in it to help drain away the blood that was pouring into his pleural cavity. In the emergency room there was a great deal of running about, and then the nurses made an effort to cover up the President's body as it lay on the bed. The cut-away clothes—scraps of fabric now, and nothing more—were taken away and deposited somewhere.

Someone else was in the same room with the President, but

he was too far off in his own dreamlike state to be conscious of much that went on around him. He was curious about why the doctors and nurses were so anxious to wipe up the blood that had leaked out into the bandages.

Then, quite suddenly, he could see through the fog of pain and he recognized Nancy in the room with him, peering down with those enormous, wide-open, expressive eyes of hers.

He could feel her concern and empathize with her fear over his safety. Instinctively he searched for the right thing to say to her—something to reassure her, something to take that intensity of pain and suffering (caused by his suffering) out of her eyes.

Often he had told people that the worst part about having something bad happen to him or to any of the members of his family was in trying to figure out how to tell Nancy about it. She took things so much more to heart than he. Over the years he had developed a way of deflecting her pain and hurt, the same way he had developed a method of deflecting pain and hurt from himself.

Humor was the weapon. He and his brother had thickened their own thin skins when they were growing up by shooting down pain through humor. It was a tradition that the Irish used humor to bear their sorrows and to dry up their tears. He and his brother, Moon—Neil—knew how helpful it was to them in their younger years.

It flashed into his mind that Jack Dempsey, another Irishman, used humor, too. Take the time he had lost his heavyweight title to Gene Tunney. With that sense of humor the Irish were so famous for, he went home to tell his wife that he had lost, but he put it this way:

"Honey, I forgot to duck."

And so now Ronald Reagan told Nancy Reagan that he too had forgotten to duck—hoping he would be able to drain off some of the worry and anxiety that was building up in her over his safety. Everything will be all right, he thought. Everything will be all right.

He was surprised now to feel her hand in his, gripping

25

his strongly, almost as if it were trying to infuse him with her own energy and lifeblood. He tried to grip her hand back, but he had no idea if his muscles had responded to his brain or not. It was very difficult to concentrate on what was happening now.

He opened his eyes again, and he could not find her. She had gone out of the room. He was still lying there, and the doctors were trying to put an intravenous tube into his jugular. He was unused to the pain, and he thrashed about on the bed in agony. Finally they gave up and he lay still, resting at last.

"Mr. President," said a voice.

He opened his eyes. There was someone there, but he could not make out who it was. He could see a face that might belong to a doctor, or to a male nurse, or to almost anyone, for that matter.

"Mr. President, there's a lot of blood coming from your chest tube."

He was unable to respond. He knew about the blood and he had guessed how he had been hurt.

"We know the bullet's in your chest."

A bullet in the chest, he thought. So it wasn't a broken rib at all. It was a bullet.

"We don't know what's injured," the voice went on.

That was just great, thought the President. The truth of the matter was that he didn't know either. Were they trying to get him to tell them what was wrong? He simply didn't know!

"Because the blood continues to come, we think it would be safest to take you to the operating room."

That made sense, certainly. But why didn't they just do it instead of indulging in all this talk?

"We don't feel you're in any immediate danger, but we think that would be the safest thing to do rather than to watch you bleed."

How could he not be in danger when he was unable to get a grip on things and even be conscious of what was going on around him?

"We simply don't know how long you can continue this way."

Nor do I, the President thought to himself. Nor do I.

Of course, he knew they were asking for his permission to operate on him. Under ordinary circumstances, he would have refused them permission. He knew his body and knew its capabilities. He had recovered from other wounds. He could recover from this.

But this situation was different. He needed the kind of technical help the hospital could give in order to survive. He opened his eyes wider to study the face looking down at him, and tried to speak—but of course he could not. Instead he nodded his head in consent.

The face peering at him understood and withdrew. It was the face of the senior surgeon at George Washington. When he was out of the President's line of vision, other faces appeared to view. Ronald Reagan recognized Mike Deaver, Ed Meese, and James Baker. They were standing in the middle distance, watching him with a great deal of concern.

Now habit took over, and Ronald Reagan took in a deep breath—no matter what it cost him to do it—and spoke out loud to them.

"Who's minding the store?" he asked them with what could almost pass for a grin.

No one said anything, but the three chief aides waved at him and tried to appear confident.

The quip had worked, the same as his quip earlier to Nancy. Once he got going, no one could stop him.

"I'd like to take this whole scene again," he told the doctor and his aides. "Beginning at the hotel entrance."

Now he heard the welcoming sound of laughter from everyone around him.

Almost immediately the haze settled down over him again, the way it had before, and he sank back with his eyes half closed. Then the bed he was on began to roll out of Bay 5A. It was actually a gurney and not a bed at all.

The institutional walls and ceiling flowed past him, and he knew he was being wheeled down a corridor somewhere. Now he could feel someone walking along beside him—someone out there in the very near space—holding tightly to his hand as he sailed along half out of his mind.

It was Nancy. He knew that. And yet he could not see her at all.

And then, as he moved along, he could hear a voice saying:

"He looks real gray. I wonder if he'll make it."

He'll make it, he told himself. He's got to. And he squeezed the hand that was gripping his so tightly. He could feel the encouragement she was trying to send to him in the clasp of her hand in return.

"Don't worry about me," he said with what he tried to make a grin. "I'll make it."

And he would. Except that he did not know whether he had thought the words or really said them out loud. He pondered the thought a long moment, wondering.

Then everything around him seemed to recede into the distance and all consciousness faded away. Only he was there. He and Nancy.

3

Love at First Sight?

Beverly Glen Boulevard is one of those narrow, leisurely, winding roadways common to Southern California that combines affluent, extensive estates with tiny warrenlike habitats. The "boulevard" itself meanders up into the Santa Monica Mountains—actually they are foothills, not mountains—from its origins somewhere south of Wilshire Boulevard, and eventually crosses the summit over into Sherman Oaks in the San Fernando Valley.

Along its sometimes picturesque twistings and turnings, shaded by eucalyptus and cottonwood trees, nestle thousands of tiny, casual, cramped-in cottages, of all different shapes, sizes, styles, and degrees of grandeur, resembling what would probably best be called "summer homes" in the more rustic areas of the country, along with huge, sumptuous estates in the very best Hollywood tradition demonstrating high status, wealth, and glamour.

In the late 1940s, "the Glen" was sometimes confusedly thought to be a part of Bel Air, and at other times was erroneously identified with Beverly Hills, Westwood, West Los Angeles, Hollywood, and even Los Angeles proper. Primarily a residential enclave, Beverly Glen was inhabited by disparate sorts of people—all the way from blue-collar workers welding airplanes at Lockheed, through university students at nearby UCLA, through professors and academics of all stripes, levels, and abilities, through some minor celebrities in the art, literary, and show-business worlds, and on up to prestigious and world-renowned figures in all walks of life.

29

With very few exceptions, much of Beverly Glen is not composed of the superbly landscaped, tenderly nurtured, and exquisitely set-out English-manor-type estates so familiar to visitors of residences belonging to Hollywood stars. Few swimming pools, tennis courts, or extensive gardens flourish here—except, of course, in the more posh and manicured sections of the Glen down south of Sunset Boulevard and close to the Wilshire Boulevard area.

It was, just after World War II, a relaxed and vital community composed mostly of intellectuals, workers, and an occasional genius of one sort or another.

Here a twenty-eight-year-old motion-picture starlet named Nancy Davis lived in a five-room, two-story apartment, from which she found it a quick and easy drive down Wilshire Boulevard to Overland, and then straight on out to Culver City and the MGM lot, where she was under standard contract as a motion-picture ingenue, or "starlet," to use the more popular term of the era.

In the fall of 1949, Nancy Davis was at work on a picture titled *East Side, West Side*, directed and produced by Mervyn LeRoy, whose *The Wizard of Oz* had already become a film classic and had established him as a major motion-picture producer and director. The picture on which Nancy Davis was at work starred Barbara Stanwyck, Ava Gardner, Cyd Charisse, Van Heflin, and James Mason. It was the third motion picture in which she had been assigned a role after signing her contract with the studio.

Nancy had come into the motion-picture business through the normal channels. She had first appeared in summer stock in the East, and had then finally made it to Broadway as a minor character in a successful musical comedy. However, she had an advantage over the average starlet, who might be forced to move upward in the industry on the devious but standard route that frequently included conversations at Schwab's Drugstore, "deals" with unknown agents, "arrangements" with producers and directors, and so on. Her mother and father were close friends of Walter Huston and his son John—Nancy knew Walter Huston as "Uncle Walter"—and the Spencer Tracys, along with other famous Hollywood luminaries.

She was looked upon by the studio executives and by her co-workers as an up-and-coming young actress, in an industry that could be extremely hard on newcomers. In spite of the good luck of her family connections and her obvious talents, Nancy Davis was considerably worried at the moment about her future career. Her name had just appeared in the *Hollywood Reporter* among a long list of "known" Communist sympathizers in the motion-picture business. She was afraid that its appearance there could mean a quick end to her career. An obvious mistake of some kind had occurred; she had no idea what was causing her to be confused with a radical sympathizer.

She felt also that the intentional or unintentional linking of her name with the Communist cause—a cause which she did not believe in and in no way supported—might somehow taint the careers of those people with whom she was on a first-name basis.

Her director, Mervyn LeRoy, was a friend of the family, and he listened to her carefully when she sought him out on the set one morning. She told him about the appearance of her name in the trade paper and about the mailings she was continuing to receive from Communist groups announcing meetings and containing propaganda newsletters.

"Somehow they seem to have gotten the idea that I'm a member of the Communist Party. I'm most certainly not."

The director told her not to worry about it. It was obviously a mistake and should lead to no difficulties.

But Nancy was not quite so sure. "I'm very upset about this," she told him. "Is there anything I can do about it? I don't want my mother and father dragged into this thing any more than I want myself hurt by it."

LeRoy thought a moment. "I know someone who can fix things up for you."

"Who?"

"The president of the Screen Actors Guild. Ronald Reagan."

Nancy knew who he was. She had seen most of his pictures. In fact, she thought he was a very personable and talented actor who had not had the right breaks to make him a superstar.

"He's been trying to weed out the real Communists in the Screen Actors Guild himself," Mervyn LeRoy went on. "Don't get me wrong. He's not on a witch hunt. He doesn't want non-Communists hurt. He wants to clear innocent people as well as get at the truth about others who aren't."

"How do I go about seeing him?" Nancy asked.

"I'll handle it," said LeRoy. "Actually, Ronnie is a very decent young man. You're a very nice young woman. It might be a good thing for you to meet."

Nancy smiled. "I've seen him in films. I think you're right about him. I *would* like to meet him."

And Nancy went back to work on the set.

In the hours that followed, she began thinking a great deal about Ronald Reagan. She had been reading in the newspapers about the breakup of his marriage to Jane Wyman—a marriage that had been "made in heaven," according to the newspaper columnists and Hollywood magazine writers. She knew that he had been president of SAG since 1947, taking over from Robert Montgomery. She knew that his work on behalf of the union had certainly not endeared him to the producers who ran the film studios.

There was talk that his career had taken a bad turn when he had gone into the service during the war. As a result of it, he had missed three years of work in front of the cameras. There was also talk about the fact that Jane Wyman's career was soaring higher and higher while Ronald Reagan's career seemed to have peaked and was plummeting to the bottom.

She found herself thinking more about him through the afternoon, and she began to wonder if he would indeed call her after he had heard about her potential problem from Mervyn LeRoy. When she got home she even contacted the telephone company to make sure there was nothing wrong with her phone. And when she did that she sat there thinking about it and about what a fool she was to do it, and she could have kicked herself for being so eager.

Nevertheless, the phone remained mute. Nancy decided to take it philosophically. She was twenty-eight years old, and she had dated a large number of presentable and even exciting men. None of them had appeared right for her. And yet, she *was* twenty-eight—an age that would be considered to make her an "old maid" in other contemporary cultures. Perhaps her worst fears were being realized. Maybe indeed life *was* going to pass her by. She glanced disapprovingly at the phone and shook her head ever so slightly.

Next day on the set, Mervyn LeRoy called her aside.

"I've got good news for you. The president of the Screen Actors Guild has checked you out."

Well, thought Nancy Davis, isn't that just dandy!

Mervyn LeRoy did not sense her feeling of annoyance. He went right on. "In fact, there are at least four Nancy Davises in show business—in motion pictures, and on the stage. He assures me that if your name comes up, the guild will defend you."

Nancy smiled and nodded her approval, trying to hide her somewhat crestfallen feelings. Didn't Mervyn LeRoy understand? She wanted to have Ronald Reagan tell her that himself! Obviously, he had misunderstood; or perhaps it was her own fault in assuming that she would be able to meet the SAG president in person.

"Oh," she said with a somewhat fragile smile, trying to mask her disappointment. "I suppose that's all right. I *am* worried, though. You know, I think it would make me feel better if he explained it to me himself."

The director eyed her with just the slightest tug of a smile working at the corner of his mouth. "I see. Well, I wouldn't want anybody working for me to be *worried*. It might affect her work on the set."

Nancy went right on, pretending the director had said nothing. "I really don't think it's *too* much for a member of an organization to ask her president to make a direct report, do you?"

LeRoy was grinning. "No, I don't think it really is. Let me see what I can do."

Whatever Mervyn LeRoy did, it worked. That same evening Nancy was sitting by the telephone, wondering if this was going to be another one of those dull, silent evenings, when it suddenly rang.

"Hello," she said into the mouthpiece in her very own reserved stage voice, very cool, very controlled.

"I'd like to speak to Nancy Davis."

"This is she."

"This is Ronald Reagan, the president of the Screen Actors Guild. At the request of a mutual friend, I've done some official work for you," he told her with that somehow familiar tone of amusement he used in his screen roles, "and I wondered if you were free for dinner this evening. We could discuss the problem then."

Nancy counted to five. Everything seemed to be breaking right at this point. "Well, it's awfully short notice," she said, "but it just so happens that I *can* manage it."

And that left the ball in his court. He played it. "Fine. But it's going to have to be a quickie dinner. I have an early call in the morning at the studio."

Nancy smiled. That was a standard ploy for anyone going out on a blind date in the industry. She knew he had no early call, and she knew that *he* knew she knew.

"Actually that's best for me too, since I too have an early call on the set tomorrow morning."

Of course Nancy had no early call either; and she knew that *he* knew.

"I'll be by about eight."

Within minutes of eight o'clock, the doorbell rang, and Nancy rose slowly to answer it. He was an instantly recognizable figure, tall, slender, and well-built—with that half-smiling Irish grin on his face and a sparkle in his blue eyes. What startled Nancy was the fact that Ronald Reagan was standing in her doorway supported by crutches.

Trying to recover her poise, she remembered reading in the

paper several months ago that he had injured himself in a charity baseball game between two groups of Hollywood actors as he slid into first base. She suddenly realized that it was extremely presumptuous of her to set up a date with him and force him to come over to pick her up while he was still seemingly on the injured list.

However, she was able to swallow her concern and smile brightly. Before she could speak, he said:

"Nancy Davis?"

"Yes." She smiled. "And that means that you're Ronald Reagan."

He stood there, apparently having no rejoinder to this rather ridiculous comment, and making no attempt to move inside.

"I'll get my coat," she said. In a moment they were descending the stairs to his car.

"I've booked us for dinner at LaRue's. That is, if it's all right with you?"

"Oh, that's fine," she said.

Of course it was fine. LaRue's was one of the most "in" of the excellent and expensive restaurants located on the Sunset Strip. She knew, in fact, that it was one of the most popular places in the Los Angeles area. At that time the Strip was the place to go and the place to be seen, and LaRue's was the place on the Strip to go and to be seen, and its dinners were among the best around.

As he drove the car down the winding road and onto Sunset Boulevard, Nancy watched him out of the corner of her eye. He was almost exactly as he appeared on the screen, she decided—nice-looking, with that fresh, open, Midwestern, all-American look.

She didn't say much. Ronnie kept the conversational ball going. He talked easily, with a natural flow of marvelous stories and quips. Nancy was somewhat surprised to note that his delivery and his speech pattern were amazingly similar to her own mother's. He had that same sparkling, effervescent way about him, with the hint of laughter bubbling up from below at the end of almost every line he spoke.

In a way, Nancy knew that it should not be surprising that Ronald Reagan and her mother resembled one another in the way they talked. After all, both were professional actors. She listened to him with a kind of déjà vu, and found his presence comfortable and stimulating to her. It was as if she were being wrapped up in a warm and charming presence that had the capability of making her happy.

Once at LaRue's, they were led to a table in the corner, and there followed the obligatory and typically technical discussion concerning the contents of the meal. Their conversation struck her as amusing and lively, especially given Ronald Reagan's lighthearted and somehow witty approach to it. She found herself giggling and answering his somewhat sly questions in an almost frivolous manner. When the waiter had left and the headwaiter had dropped by to say hello to Ronald Reagan, they sat there for several moments in a companionable and somehow intimate silence.

Then Ronald Reagan immediately approached the problem that had led the two of them to this meeting.

"I checked out the guild files the other day after I heard what was bothering you. I suppose you'll be pleased to know that there are at least four Nancy Davises in show business."

"Four!" Nancy was properly stunned.

"Four is too many," he said matter-of-factly. "That leads me to a suggestion that may solve your dilemma."

"And what is that?"

"Have the studio change your name."

"But it *is* my name! I'm Nancy Davis and I always have been!"

He swallowed quickly. "Oh. I thought the studio publicity department had given it to you. Sorry." He was smiling ruefully. Suddenly his eyes twinkled. "In that case perhaps you may *not* be too pleased to learn there are four Nancy Davises. In fact, it is probably somewhat of a shock to learn that there are three other people out there pretending to be you."

Nancy smiled. "Oh well, I don't mind as long as they behave themselves. It's when they *don't* that I worry."

"That's the point, of course," he said. "At least one of them may not be behaving herself. That's the one you have to watch out for."

"Is there anything I can do about *that* Nancy Davis?" she asked.

"I don't think so, really. But not to worry, as the English say. If a problem ever arises over something one of the other Nancy Davises does, you must let me know immediately, and the guild will take care of it as soon as possible."

And that was that.

With that "important" business out of the way, the conversation took a somewhat different turn. Although Nancy found herself saying little, she was quite attentive to every word her escort said. The first thing she noticed about him was that although Ronald Reagan was a successful, well-known, and highly paid movie actor, he did not talk exclusively about acting, or about the movie he was working on at the time or was about to make, or about the things that were going on in the industry. The conversation seemed to move quite gracefully into other areas.

Fox example, she was surprised to learn that he owned a small ranch out in the San Fernando Valley. He even kept a number of horses there. He began telling her about riding, and she told him that she did not know much about riding. She *had* ridden, of course, but it was not one of her most common forms of recreation.

His eyes sparkled. "Well, actually, I don't do much riding now, either. I've still got these crutches to contend with."

"I read in the paper somewhere that you broke your leg sliding into first base," Nancy said with one eyebrow quirked slightly upward.

He shook his head with a groan. "I saw that story in the paper myself. It's the most foolish thing I ever heard of. Nobody *slides* into first base. What would be the point?"

He was right. She knew that there was no need to slide into first. You slid into second, or third, or into home plate, where you could be tagged out.

37

"How *did* it happen?" she asked. "I had wondered about that."

His eyes lit up. "You like baseball?"

"Of course," Nancy said. "I like to watch it, not play it. Now, how *did* you break your leg?"

"Actually, I just ran into the first baseman with all stops open. My leg simply came apart like a wet cigar." He sat there shaking his head in disbelief at the memory of it.

"Simply came apart?" Nancy repeated. "But how?"

He sighed and then smiled briefly. "Eddie Bracken set up this Movie Star World Series—softball, of course—in order to raise money for the City of Hope Hospital. That's a charity, you know—one the Hollywood community likes to support. His idea was to have the comedians in the industry go up against the leading men. Actually some of the comedians are bigger leading men than the so-called leading men. I was busy and didn't really intend to participate. But just before the game was sheduled to be played down at Wrigley Field in Los Angeles, I stopped at a traffic light in Beverly Hills and right next to me Eddie Bracken rolled up and looked over at me. That was when I remembered that he had asked me to play and I had kind of stalled him about it.

" 'You're playing in the game, aren't you, Ronnie?' he asked me.

"Well, he had me there, trapped at the stoplight. What could I say but yes? So the day of the game—it was Sunday evening—there I was with all the rest of them, down at Wrigley Field in L.A."

He looked up with a sudden grin. "It takes me a long time to get to the point, doesn't it?"

Nancy laughed. "You're just like my mother. Of course it takes you a long time to get to the point. But getting there's sometimes the best part!"

He shrugged. "Anyway, the game began with the comedians in the field and the leading men up to bat. Bracken decided to make me the lead-off batter. I warned him I wasn't all that good, but he said he knew I could ride a horse better than he could and that made me a good bet for leading off the batting order."

Nancy laughed. "I don't quite follow the logic of that, but go on."

"There's no logic to it. Anyway, there I was, swinging the bat and looking out into the field, thinking about Babe Ruth pointing to the right-field stands, and the game began. Bob Hope was pitching and Ward Bond was catching. I was scheduled for the infield somewhere. I never got a chance to find out what position I was supposed to play. Bill Demerest was umpiring, and he called two balls and one strike on me. Then Hope lobbed over an easy pitch and I had this bright idea to bunt the ball. I did, and I ran hard for first base and there was a lot of scrambling around by the players. Somebody tossed the ball to the first baseman. He hogged the bag to block me off, and I slammed into him. Anyway, that was it."

There was a silence for a moment. His eyes seemed to be shadowed with pain.

"What can I say? I was running along like a real pro ballplayer and—I fell apart! I tried to get up but couldn't. I was in terrible pain. Of course, they X-rayed me later at the hospital, and I had broken my leg. In fact, I had a comminuted fracture in six places!"

Nancy suppressed whatever amusement she might have been feeling, and watched him as he slowly smiled.

"Let me tell you," he said with a shake of the head, "it was the most ignominious exit I ever made! I was carried bodily off the field—the most ridiculous thing that ever happened to me. I was more embarrassed than anything else. Embarrassed and mad! I mean, here I was, scheduled to make a picture with Ida Lupino at Universal, and I couldn't even get up and walk!"

Nancy nodded sympathetically.

"The newspaper items didn't help any either when they wrote that I had injured myself 'sliding into first.' Nobody but a dodo would do that. Don't those writers ever see a baseball game?"

There was a moment of silence and then he looked up at her, his eyes slightly narrowed as if he were in pain.

"You know, I was in the hospital for eight weeks, in a cast, and nobody from Warner Brothers Studio ever showed up to find out how I was or even to say hello."

He looked down at his empty plate.

"Oh, well, that's not your problem. In fact, it isn't even my problem. I sometimes wonder what these Hollywood producers are made of."

Nancy could feel his hurt and understand his sense of rejection. Instantly she realized that he was not only feeling miserable because of the way his studio had treated him, but possibly experiencing a resurgence of the emotional turmoil he had gone through when he was separating from Jane Wyman and his two children.

Skillfully, Nancy broke in and said: "Weren't you in England recently making a movie version of some hit play?"

Ronald Reagan looked up. *"The Hasty Heart.* It was all Richard Todd's picture. He's a great one, and it's a good part. In fact, it's a good play—a fine picture, and I hope it does well."

"How did you like England? I've never been there."

"It was terrible," he said. "I liked the people, but the weather was just awful! We were there four months, and the food absolutely drove me crazy. You just can't eat it! Do you know, I hade to send over to '21' in New York for a dozen steaks to try to get me through the week. Actually, I only got to eat two of them. The refrigeration at the Savoy Hotel was so bad the rest of them spoiled."

He chuckled good-naturedly. "Oh, I'm probably making that up. The food was fine—*if* you're English! The first time I ate at the Savoy I ordered pheasant under glass. Now, that's a real treat for a gourmet! At least, so I had thought. I ordered it and . . ." He shook his head in disbelief. "They served me this bird, complete with feathered ruff and head and yellow legs!"

Nancy tried to smother her laughter.

"I looked at the bird, and it looked right back at me. Somehow it seemed that if I touched that bird with a fork, it would scream out in pain. I couldn't eat it. I gave up right then and there."

A moment later Ronald Reagan was talking about the monetary situation. American funds were frozen in England at the time, the English being under a self-enforced "austerity" plan instituted by their Labour government. That was the reason Warner Brothers had decided to shoot a picture in England—using the money that the company could not get out of the country.

"I thought it was an imposition," he said. "I couldn't take my money out of there either. And I needed it. Nevertheless, it was a wonderful place. To visit."

The conversation picked up again as he told her about places he had seen in England, and reminisced about many of the things he had liked about the country. Then he told her how he had gone to Dublin to take part with other American actors in a special Royal Command Performance, and later had traveled to France and the Riviera. He had even won money at Monte Carlo.

"What a stack of francs I raked in—just like in the movies." He chuckled. "It looked like a grand haul—I was the man who broke the bank at Monte Carlo."

"How much did you win?" Nancy couldn't help asking.

"By the time we got all those thousands of francs translated into American dollars, I had about"—he glanced at her with a wink—"sixty-five dollars, give or take a quarter."

Nancy was laughing again.

"I didn't know the franc was selling for two cents during the war," he added with a self-mocking grin. Then he stopped smiling and looked at her steadily.

She straightened. "What's the matter? Is there something wrong with me?"

He shook his head. "Not a thing that I can see. It's that absolutely wonderful laugh of yours! I've never heard anything to equal it!"

And of course she laughed again. He smiled, listening.

From there the talk drifted over to other subjects, including a rather long and involved explanation of his negotiations with the studio bosses as head of the Screen Actors Guild. He had a great deal to say about the union and about the people with whom he worked on the executive board.

He asked Nancy about herself, and when she tried to guide him back into his ordinary line of chatter, he concentrated on her parents. What did her father do? What did her mother do?

Nancy was not prepared to talk much on the subject of herself, but she did begin to talk about her mother and father. Ronald Reagan learned almost immediately that Nancy Davis's father was probably the most famous and talented surgeon in the country, and that her mother had been one of the stage's best actresses before she retired from the theater.

Without quite realizing it, Nancy was going along at a great rate of speed when suddenly she was brought up short by a question that seemed to come at her out of the thin air.

"Who did you say?" he was asking her.

"Uncle Walter."

"But isn't that . . ." Ronald Reagan's face went blank. "Isn't that Walter *Huston?*"

"Well, of course it is," Nancy said. "Who did you think it was? I thought I *told* you—"

"I thought you were a starlet over at MGM," he said with a half-smile. "I didn't know you were intimate with people like Walter Huston!"

"My mother acted with him on the stage." She giggled, and Ronald Reagan leaned back in his chair and savored the sound of it. "When I was a teenager I used to come out to spend some of the summer days with Uncle Walter. He was going to do a play on Broadway. There was a producer there named Josh Logan."

Without a word Ronald Reagan threw up his hands in mock astonishment. "A producer named Josh Logan," he seemed to be saying. "*The* Josh Logan, more than likely."

Nancy went right on. "He wanted Uncle Walter to do a musical! Now, I knew Uncle Walter and I knew he had a tin ear and couldn't sing a note. When he asked me my advice about the role, I told him it wasn't for him at all. I told him I didn't think he would be happy acting and trying to sing too. It would expose his inability to carry a tune and drive the audience away from the theater."

Ronald Reagan cocked an eyebrow at her. "You told him that? And he took your advice?"

"Of course not!" Nancy chuckled. "He ignored my advice and signed up for the part. It was the part of Peter Stuyvesant in *Knickerbocker Holiday!* His rendition of 'September Song' became a classic."

Ronald Regan threw his head back and laughed so loudly a number of patrons at LaRue's looked over at him with some puzzlement.

"That's not the end of the story," said Nancy. "After the musical went down in history as a classic, Uncle Walter gave me a copy of the printed version in book form with a note on the title page: 'To Nancy, who told me to do it.' "

Ronald Regan smiled. "An uncle who's one of the top actors in the industry, a father who's the best surgeon in the United States, bar none, and a mother who was the greatest actress of her day." Something occurred to him. "Who's your godfather, anyway? Who's looking after you?"

"If I haven't a godfather, I do have a godmother. It's Alla Nazimova."

He threw up his hands in total surrender. "I knew it had to be someone like that! At *least* Alla Nazimova."

Nancy found herself giggling again. "I sound like a name-dropper of the worst sort, don't I?"

"Next you'll be telling me you've been dating Clark Gable or Spencer Tracy."

Her face turned pink. "But I *have* dated Clark Gable, and I *do* know Spencer Tracy. Spence is a friend of my mother's and acted with her in a number of plays before he went to Hollywood."

Ronald Reagan simply stared at her, shaking his head in amazement.

43

Nancy was embarrassed. She decided not to talk so much. "I want to know more about *you*," she told him. "There's plenty of time to talk about me."

Ronald Reagan grinned and began tossing out lines to make her laugh. Conversation drifted, and soon he was reminiscing about his work with the special branch of the armed forces he had served in during the war. He had been stationed in Hollywood, and never served in combat. It was almost as if he were embarrassed by the whole episode. He had understood and sympathized with her embarrassment a moment before, and now she understood and sympathized with his. Adroitly—almost without his knowledge—she guided the conversation in her usual low-keyed and unobtrusive way far from the war and his part in it, letting him take the lead and travel in any direction he pleased.

Suddenly he looked at her and said: "Hey, have you ever been to see Sophie Tucker perform?"

"No," Nancy answered, "I haven't. But I've heard many of her records. And I enjoy her singing immensely."

Ronald Reagan's eyes lit up. "She's opening right down the street tonight at Ciro's, you know."

Nancy nodded. "I think I did see a notice of that in the paper."

He reached across the table and gripped her hand. "Let's wrap it up here and go down to see her!"

Before she could answer, he had waved his hand at the waiter for the bill.

"What about your early call tomorrow morning?" Nancy asked with a faint smile.

"Don't worry about it. I'll make it." He grinned right back, knowing that neither one of them had an early call the following morning.

They drove down the Strip to Ciro's nearby and hurried in just in time to catch Sophie Tucker's first show. They sat there in the nightclub, absorbed in each other, and breaking off momentarily to watch the show as it proceeded. They continued sitting there as it went on, and when it had finished, they were still sitting there totally absorbed. They were talking to each other in quiet, intimate tones when the second show began. They sat through that one too. When the third and last show ended, they finally left the nightclub and started back for Beverly Glen Boulevard.

He said good night to her at her front door. At that point Nancy discovered that it was three in the morning. She was astonished. It was not like her to stay out so late, but it was particularly surprising for her to do so without even being aware of how much time had elapsed.

She watched him as he left, tottering down the steps on his crutches, but not before he had made her promise to go out with him again, even though there was no problem for him or for the guild to solve.

Looking back on that night many years later, Nancy wrote in her autobiography:

"I don't know if it was love at first sight, but it was something close to it. We were taken with one another and wanted to see more of each other. We had dinner the next night and the night after that and the night after that. We took in all the shows at all the clubs, and there were a lot of clubs in those days. We saw all the Sophie Tuckers I had missed in my life. As soon as we realized that a steady diet of night life wasn't what we really wanted, we started to have quiet evenings."

Without quite realizing it in the days and nights that followed, the two of them became a special part of each other's life—special and very important. In their own low-keyed way, however, neither of them made a great deal out of it in words spoken aloud. Each preserved that roped-off area in the heart against trespassing. Their feeling for each other was a very real, very true thing. Their close friends knew what was going on in the important relationship between them, but their professional associates in the industry—even though they may have sensed it—did not make it common knowledge.

And they learned almost everything there was to learn about each other—and as they learned those details, their affection for each other grew into an everlasting and indestructible feeling.

4

One for the Gipper

The fortieth President of the United States was born on February 11, 1911, in a cramped, tiny flat above a general store in the small Illinois town of Tampico, located about 125 miles west of Chicago. Ronald Wilson Reagan's father, Jack Edward Reagan, sold shoes in the H. C. Pitney General Store located below the family rooms.

Ronald was the second son of the Reagans. His brother Neil—nicknamed "Moon" in the early months of his life—was two years older than he. When Jack Reagan saw his second-born screaming his head off in the arms of his mother, he said: "For such a little bit of a Dutchman, he makes a lot of noise, doesn't he?"

And the name "Dutch" stuck to young Ronald Reagan through his youth and early manhood, just as the name "Moon" stuck to his brother.

The two adult Reagans were obvious contrasts. Jack Reagan was the son of a transplanted Irish Catholic who had lapsed from Catholicism to marry a Protestant girl in America. Nelle Wilson Reagan came from a Scots-English background, and ran the family with a firm but loving hand. She had to. Her husband was a hard worker, a heavy drinker, and a deep cynic. Nelle Wilson was an idealist, and she believed the best of people and thought that if she loved everyone, everyone would love her.

Jack Reagan was an ingrained pessimist and Nelle Wilson an unreconstructed optimist, and they always seemed to be on a collision course, yet their marriage lasted without threat of collapse throughout their lives.

It was from his mother that Ronald got not only his love of people but an early taste for the theater. Nelle Reagan was known throughout every neighborhood she lived in for her charitable efforts. In addition to that, she was devoted to amateur dramatics and frequently put on public recitals for everyone to attend.

Before a performance it was not unusual for the group to come to the Reagans' flat to rehearse for a play scheduled for production at the Tampico Opera House—an upstairs "theater" capable of seating about two hundred enthusiastic local theatergoers. Ronald was sometimes pressed into service—once he even played a character in a Sunday-school pageant named *The Spirit of Christmas That Never Was.*

As for his father, Ronald Reagan always remembered him as "a typical Irishman"—happy-go-lucky, sensitive, jolly, companionable, but at the same time unfortunately weak. He had what his son later referred to as "the Irish disease"—a predilection for whiskey. But because he was personable, affable, and loaded with charisma, he was a good salesman and was usually able to land a job working as a clerk in a department store. Shoes were his specialty.

The family moved around frequently during Ronald's early years. When he was two years old, they lived in Chicago, where Jack Reagan worked at Marshall Field's department store. The house in which they stayed in South Chicago was illuminated by gas—or at least it was when the Reagans had the quarter to pay to turn it on. The job there lasted for two years, and then Jack Reagan pulled up stakes and moved on to Galesburg, Illinois. After Galesburg, there was Monmouth, then Tampico again, and finally, when Ronald was nine, the family more or less settled down in Dixon, a town on the Rock River about ninety miles from Chicago. There Jack Reagan finally opened his own shoe store, the Jack Reagan Fashion Boot Shop. Dixon came to be what Dutch considered his hometown.

Although the 1920s meant unparalleled prosperity for most Americans, the life of ease did not seem to trickle down to the citizens of Dixon and its environs. Sometimes it was difficult to make enough money to buy food and pay the rent, and there were some meals that were a bit lean.

The big meal of the week was Sunday night—calves' liver and fried onions. The rest of the week Nelle Reagan would put a soup bone in a big pot, chop up some carrots and potatoes, pour in some water, and feed the family on that until the following Sunday. Ronald could remember how his mother kept adding water and carrots and potatoes to the pot as the mixture continued to lose its potency every weekday.

And yet Nelle Reagan was a woman of great religious faith. When someone would remind her that the rent was due and that there was no money to pay for it, she would obstinately say:

"Don't worry about it. The Lord will provide."

And somehow the Lord, or something or someone, did provide.

Five years after arriving in Dixon, Dutch Reagan entered North Dixon High School. He was no student; he simply wasn't interested in books and papers, although he could read rapidly and had no trouble scoring on tests. He concentrated on sports—playing basketball and football, participating in track meets, and serving as president of the student body.

In his later years someone once asked him why he had not been more successful as a student in school with his obvious ability to read and take tests.

"Heck," he said. "I knew if I got a lot of good grades, I'd be automatically categorized as an intellectual and a teacher type. I certainly didn't want to be a teacher!"

He also sensed that it was the athlete who was popular with his fellow students, and not the book reader.

In spite of his seeming obsession with sports, he was not successful on the field when he first entered high school. The fact of the matter was that he was a runt—five feet three inches, weighing about 108 pounds "with weights in my pockets," as he put it. Every year, as sure as clockwork, he tried to make the high school football team and failed—until he was in his third year. Then, finally, they let him start out the games as a member of the first team.

The problem was that he was too nearsighted to run out for passes or throw passes to players in the field. He could not clearly see either the ball or the players. What he ended up doing was playing guard on the line, pushing and bumping heads with the opposition players. He didn't need 20/20 vision for that—in fact, the less he saw at guard, the better.

He also found plenty of time to take part in high school dramatics and other theatrical ventures. He found he was good at it, had an excellent voice, and knew how to deliver lines in a natural and compelling way.

Ronald Reagan had an antipathy to pursuing a career as a teacher and so he was not totally absorbed in his high school studies. Yet he did not have any trouble in class. From the beginning, Dutch Reagan was what show business calls a "quick study." He had a facility for speed-reading and for instant memorization. In school he was able with little effort to acquire sufficient comprehension and knowlege of all the subjects to get by.

In spite of his feelings about teachers, he was always motivated toward a college education. He knew that it cost money to go to college, but he was determined to do so even if family funds for higher education were nonexistent. It meant that Dutch would have to go to work to earn enough money to get his college degree.

During the summers he got jobs at construction camps, earning about $35 for a sixty-hour work week. He also became a paid lifeguard at Lowell Park, a nearby resort on the Rock River, for which he earned about $15 a week. He rescued some seventy-seven people during the summers he worked there, although many of them somewhat resented being pulled out of the river, claiming they were not really in any danger of drowning. At least, so the story went.

By the time he had finished high school, Dutch Reagan had

put aside enough money to continue his education at Eureka College, near Peoria, Illinois. The town of Eureka had a motto hanging up on the main street that anyone driving through it could see: "City on the Go—with Young Men on the Go."

Eureka College itself was run by the Disciples of Christ, a tightly puritanical religious group. It was a poor, struggling little institution, handcuffed by tradition and discipline. Both Ronald and his brother, Neil, went there.

The coeducational institution had facilities for about 250 students. Dutch loved its red brick buildings, with their clean, white-framed windows—a kind of stylized American Georgian architecture. The walls were even covered with ivy and shaded by huge elms overhead.

Dutch's savings from his summer jobs were not enough to pay for his tuition, which came to $180 a year—about one-half of everything he had saved in seven years—but he was able to get a sports scholarship from the school for half his expenses, and he washed dishes and waited on tables at the Teke House—Tau Kappa Epsilon fraternity, to which he was pledged as a freshman—for the balance. He also got a job as swimming coach for the college's swimming team, worked as a lifeguard at the college pool, and even did chores in the kitchen of the girls' dormitory.

At this time Ronald Reagan was a tallish, slender, open-faced young man with stiff close-cropped hair combed with a straight part exactly in the middle of his head, and horn-rimmed glasses worn to correct his miserable eyesight. He was an outgoing, friendly, and very personable fellow.

At Eureka, he majored in economics and sociology, with a minor in dramatics, but once again he didn't really concentrate on studies. One professor even said about him:

"I know Ronald doesn't crack a book. But when it comes to tests, he writes a good test—so what can I do?"

One of Dutch Reagan's first brushes with politics—in a microcosmic sense—occurred during his freshman year. Eureka was having financial problems as well as morale problems. In order to balance the school's budget, its hard-nosed and resolute president decided to effect a number of academic cutbacks to save money. These cutbacks included a reduction in the faculty and the combining of certain departments and the elimination of others. It was already a small and threadbare school with a thin curriculum, and such a move would obviously have stripped it almost naked.

Nevertheless, the president made the decision and pushed it through the board. The students were suddenly up in arms. It was at this point that Ronald Reagan joined the freshman class at the college. There was talk among the students about the problem. They decided to fight back by going on strike against the college administration.

A petition protesting the move made by the president and the administration was signed by 143 of the 250 students. When the administration refused to act on the petition, the students all met in the chapel. It was freshman Ronald Reagan who offered the resolution to the student body to go on strike against the moves of the administration. He was a good speaker and he fired up the crowd. The resolution was passed. The students were on strike.

Dutch Reagan was one of the organizers and leaders in the strike, although he had done nothing like that before in his life. He helped rally his fellow students from his obscure position as representative of the freshman class. He even put together a series of well-thought-out petitions that went to the college's board of directors from time to time. Of course, the teachers and the students were hand-in-glove in this venture; they stuck together to the end.

Yet the whole matter was carried out in an orderly and peaceful manner. As a result of the student strike, the president of Eureka College was forced to resign and was replaced by a more liberal and enlightened man.

During college, Dutch Reagan had a lot of fun. He went out for everything: football, the student newspaper, the yearbook, the debating team. He was even cheerleader for the basketball team and was the school's best swimmer.

Largely because of his drama work in high school he became

a member of the Eureka Drama Society and acted in a number of plays. EDS enrolled in Northwestern University's one-act-play contest every year. During Dutch's senior year, the group gave a performance of *Aria da Campo*, Edna St. Vincent Millay's play about the futility of war. The group just barely missed winning first place in the contest. They did win second place, and Ronald Reagan won an individual honors trophy. He felt that he had definitely achieved "something" in dramatics.

By the time Dutch Reagan graduated with a B.A. in sociology in 1932, he had decided that his future lay in one of two directions: sports or drama. Unfortunately, luck was not entirely with him. He discovered himself, along with all his college classmates, cast adrift in the middle of the country's worst depression. His father had been forced to close up the Jack Reagan Fashion Boot Shop, and his mother had taken a $14-a-week job as a seamstress. The Great Depression was running rampant over the country. Everywhere there was big trouble.

Jack Reagan and Neil were working for the government's Works Progress Administration in Dixon.

Dutch had other plans.

In the late summer of 1932, he left Dixon for Chicago, which at the time was a major center of American radio. He loved sports and he was articulate. By putting the two talents together, he thought he had enough skill and enterprise to become a sports announcer. With almost no money in his pocket, he set out to break into radio on his own, starting out with NBC, moving on to CBS, and then on down the line to the big independent stations that were located in the Windy City.

A secretary at one of the independents was taken with Dutch's low-profile personality and good looks. She advised him not to try to break into broadcasting in Chicago, but to get a job in a smaller station somewhere out in the countryside and work his way up. She told him that the small outfits were always looking for people with good voices.

Wearily Dutch thumbed his way back to Dixon, admitting

defeat to his family. However, for once Jack Reagan was not on the down side. He had an idea. He suggested that his son map out the area around Dixon, take the family car, and start targeting all the small radio stations around the area.

And so Dutch borrowed the family car and began his search. One of the first towns he visited was Davenport, Iowa. Through a fluke the founder of radio station WOC, a chiropractor who also owned a station in Des Moines, needed an announcer. In fact, station WOC had been advertising for tryouts for a new announcer for weeks. The auditions had already been held and the candidate selected.

When Dutch Reagan strolled into WOC and asked to see the program director, he met Peter MacArthur, a transplanted Scotsman who had once worked on the stage with Harry Lauder in England. MacArthur spoke with a Scots burr that Dutch Reagan could hardly believe when he heard it. But he told the station manager why he had come.

The Scotsman almost went through the roof. "Where have ye been? Don't ye ever listen to the radio?"

Dutch though it impolitic to tell MacArthur that he never listened to WOC, and so remained silent. Then he was told that the auditions had already been held and a new announcer hired. But for some reason the Scotsman took a shine to him anyway.

Meanwhile, Dutch was doing a slow burn. Usually an equable, good-natured, and affable person, he suddenly began seething at the injustice of it. Finally he wheeled about and started to stalk out of the station. But before he opened the door he unloaded a parting shot directly at the Scotsman who had already told him off in no uncertain terms.

"How does a guy ever get to be a sports announcer if he can't get inside a station?"

It was not Dutch's temper that won him the job. It was his use of the magic phrase "sports announcer" that caught the old man's ears.

"And what was it ye said about sports?" MacArthur asked in his fuzzy burr.

"I'd like to be a sports announcer—if I can ever get a start anywhere," Dutch told him.

"And would ye perhaps know football?"

"I played football for eight years," Dutch said, mentally crossing his fingers and adding up all his time on the scrub team, in the second string, and even prime time on the bench.

"Can ye do a play-by-play to make me see a game?"

"I think I could," Dutch assured him.

With that, the transplanted associate of Harry Lauder guided him into an empty studio and sat him in front of a microphone.

"That thing in front of you is a microphone. When that red light goes on, tell me about a game, and make me *see* it."

Dutch Reagan cast his mind back to one of the most exciting games he had seen at Eureka. It was the fourth quarter of the contest against Western State University the previous year.

He grinned, remembered the time he had acted as an off-stage radio announcer for a play presented at Eureka, and began:

"How do you do, ladies and gentlemen. We are going into the fourth quarter now. We are speaking to you from high atop the Memorial Stadium of the University of Iowa, looking down from the west on the south forty-yard line. A chill wind is blowing in through the end of the stadium, and the long blue shadows are settling over the field."

From there on, he described as best he could the actual details of the game, becoming so wrapped up in the excitement of the recollection that he failed to notice MacArthur's reactions.

Twenty minutes later he wound up the game and concluded: "And now we return you to our main studio."

Dutch was almost startled when MacArthur came into the studio with a big grin on his face. "Great! Now look. We have a sponsor for four University of Iowa games. I'll give ye five dollars and bus fare if ye come in here a week from Saturday. If ye do good on that one ye can do the other three."

After the first game, MacArthur raised Dutch's pay to $10 a game and hired him for the month. Quite soon he was signed on at WOC for the somewhat stupendous salary of $100 a month—a princely sum during those Depression years.

From WOC Reagan was transferred to WHO in Des Moines, an NBC network station, and it was there that the young announcer began to be heard from coast to coast on top sports broadcasts. He announced some of the very popular Big Ten football games and covered big-league baseball games as well.

He was also learning the radio business from the ground up. Occasionally he would be assigned by the station to interview various personalities, and it was in Des Moines that he first met Joy Hodges, a singer who later became a member of Jimmy Grier's Orchestra. Largely because of her public exposure with the band, she was given a screen test and appeared in a number of short subjects at MGM. She was even considered an upcoming starlet.

When he interviewed her on the air, Dutch Reagan began his conversation with a typical throwaway line:

"Well, Miss Hodges," he said with a big grin, "how does it feel to be a movie star?"

The singer responded with an ad-libbed line that came back to haunt her in later years. "Well, Mr. Reagan," she said, giving him exactly what he had given her, "you just may know someday."

The rest of the interview was routine, and neither one of them thought much about what Joy Hodges had said to him. For the time being, anyway.

By 1937, five years after he had broken into radio, Dutch Reagan was covering all manner of sports events, including the Chicago Cubs in their spring training camp, which was at that time located on Santa Catalina Island, just off the California Coast. P. K. Wrigley, the club's owner, to all intents and purposes owned the island.

Dutch Reagan was off-duty one night and happened to visit the Biltmore Bowl at the Biltmore Hotel in Los Angeles. And there was Joy Hodges, singing with the band. Dutch scrawled a note to the singer and had it handed to her as she walked off the bandstand during intermission. She remembered him, of course, and came over to talk to him at his table. They had a long conversation between numbers, and it was during this conversation that Dutch Reagan again mentioned Joy Hodges's motion-picture career.

They were talking about the movie business when Dutch mentioned that he had never really seen the inside of a motion-picture studio. Was it possible, he asked her, to go through one of the studios?

"It's possible. The studios are pretty particular. They don't want people wandering around when they're shooting."

"Actually," Dutch Reagan admitted, "I was thinking about what you said a long time ago. If you really want to know, I'd like to get a screen test."

"Stand up," said Joy Hodges.

Puzzled, Dutch stood by the table.

"Take off those glasses."

He did so, smiling in embarrassment. "Aren't they terrible-looking?"

She nodded. "Don't ever put them on again."

"Joy," he said in despair, "I *have* to wear them! I can't see a thing without them!"

"You'll have to learn to get around," she told him. "You can't wear glasses in the movies!"

"Well," he muttered, "I suppose . . ."

"Just try to keep from bumping into things."

"Well," he laughed, "I don't know anybody in the movie business anyway. It's contacts that get you jobs out here."

"I've got an agent," Joy Hodges told him. "George Ward. He works for the Bill Meiklejohn Agency. You let me call him. How long are you going to be in town?"

She was as good as her word. She arranged for him to meet Ward the next morning, and Ward took a long hard look at Dutch Reagan, questioned him a bit about his theatrical experience, mostly to get some idea of how he talked, and then picked up the telephone.

As Dutch watched him, he dialed a number and asked for a man named Max Arnow.

Dutch Reagan didn't know Max Arnow from Hoot Gibson, and George Ward knew it. He shielded the mouthpiece and spoke to Dutch: "Max is the only casting director in town who has the power to say yes or no."

Someone answered, and the agent swung around in his chair. "Max, I've got another Robert Taylor sitting right in my office with me."

Even Dutch could hear the unbelieving cry on the wire: "God only made one Robert Taylor!"

There was some more chitchat and then Ward hung up. Swinging back around to face Dutch, he then informed the young sportscaster that he would be tested on the following Tuesday at Warner Brothers Film Studio.

When Max Arnow, the casting director at Warners, saw Ronald Reagan, he conversed with him briefly, and finally nodded. He then gave him a scene from Philip Barry's play *Holiday* to read. Dutch Reagan immediately informed Joy Hodges, who helped him rehearse the scene over the weekend.

The test was made, and Arnow told Dutch Reagan to wait around until Jack L. Warner, the studio head, returned from a trip East to view it. Reagan shook his head and told Arnow that he had to get back to Des Moines and his radio job. And he left town.

He was at work at the station when he got a wire from Warner Brothers offering him a starting wage of $200 a week.

On June 1, 1937, the film career of Ronald Reagan began. That was the day he took on the role of Andy McLeod, a radio announcer in *Love Is on the Air*, a "B" or "program" picture. An amateur in the picture business, Ronald Reagan had been assigned the *lead* in a film! His entry into the motion-picture business was smooth, quick, and without any of the usual traumas suffered by actors who were just starting up.

Furthermore, he had amazing luck with the critics. Even though the movie was purely a B work, the reviewers treated him kindly and did not comment on the fact that he seemed new and inexperienced at the game.

Although he was not aware of it at the time, Warners had been looking for someone to replace an actor named Ross Alexander who had recently committed suicide. And Ronald Reagan, with his easygoing manner, his typically American good looks, and his golden-boy charisma, fitted the bill perfectly. Once his first effort was screened and proved successful, he was "in."

In his second picture, *Hollywood Hotel*, he did not fare quite so well. He played a member of Louella Parsons's radio staff, and somehow he did not even get billing. But he was playing with such names as Dick Powell, Frances Langford, Edgar Kennedy, Benny Goodman, two of the Lane sisters (Rosemary and Lola), Ted Healy, Glenda Farrell, and the usual "cast of thousands."

Then he did a small part in an action picture called *Submarine D-1* and found the part entirely cut out from the final print. The studio kept him busy—with a vengeance. In 1938 he appeared in eight motion pictures—some Bs and some As. He appeared with Humphrey Bogart, Pat O'Brien, Ann Sheridan, Jeffrey Lynn, Edward G. Robinson, Claire Trevor, Donald Crisp, Ward Bond, James Cagney, Marie Wilson, Eddie Albert, Ralph Bellamy, Frank McHugh, Allen Jenkins, Susan Hayward, and many others.

He learned his craft quickly and well. Warner Brothers in those days was run exactly like a factory—a very well-tooled factory—with all the technical innovations of the time and none of the humanity.

It was inherent in Dutch Reagan's personality that he should consider himself very clearly a working apprentice, and not a genius who would immediately shoot to the top. Not only did he like working up the hard way but he thrived on it—and he was good at it as well.

To start with, he had an excellent speaking voice, gained in those five years during which he had learned his trade on the air waves. But it was his personality—his smiling, gracious, it's-good-to-be-alive manner—that really put him across. And it impressed the public as well as the studio bosses.

There was the good life, as well. When he started, he was making $200 a week; within two years, his agent was able to raise him to $500 a week.

One of the first dozen or so pictures he acted in was the screen version of a very funny stage farce about military schools: *Brother Rat.* Opposite him in the cast was an actress named Jane Wyman. Shortly after the completion of the film, they announced their engagement, and they were married in January 1940.

Jane Wyman had been married twice before. During their marriage, the Reagans had two children: Maureen Elizabeth and an adopted boy named Michael Edward.

The motion pictures came thick and fast—some good, some bad, some indifferent, some totally forgettable. One of his favorites during the early years was *Knute Rockne—All American,* in which he played the role of the fated-to-die George Gipp. This was a typical 1940s "adaptation" of a real-life hero's story—that of Knute Rockne, the famed Notre Dame football coach.

It was a picture that did not garner many kudos from the critics, but it was popular with the public, and it established the actor who played the ill-fated "Gipper" in the minds of the public. He was sympathetic, sensitive, and good—and yet doomed to die.

The role was actually a springboard for a wider variety of parts in other pictures. Ronald Reagan was beginning to get at least a little bit away from the type of role he had been forced to play in the beginning, the fast-talking, wise-cracking, hard-driving newspaper journalist.

In 1940–41 Ronald Reagan was chosen in the exhibitors' poll "Stars of Tomorrow" as one of the five new players of the season who were most likely to emerge as stars in the future. Yet in most of his movies he played the role of the pleasant American hero.

In 1941 the studio brass assigned the part of Drake McHugh

in Henry Bellamann's novel *King's Row* to Ronald Reagan. He did not star in the picture, but in years that followed its release, he was the one most remembered of the cast. The story itself was a brooding, moody study of a group of inbred, self-tortured, and unstable people. Hints of euthanasia, homosexuality, and even incest occurred in scene after scene. Sadistic and masochistic behavior motivated many of the characters. Dr. Tower and his daughter Cassandra were obvious candidates for the psycho ward; actually, the scriptwriters were forced to delete any references to incest and play it as a more acceptable foible, simple insanity.

The most shocking and memorable scene in the novel came over even more vividly in the motion picture. Dr. Henry Gordon, played by Charles Coburn, disliked Drake McHugh for his reckless, playboy ways. When Drake, played by Ronald Reagan, was injured in a railyard accident, Gordon amputated both his legs—as a kind of punishment for Drake McHugh's hedonistic attitude toward life.

Drake woke up in bed to find that he had no legs and cried out in horror:

"Where's the rest of me?"

An unforgettable moment. An unforgettable picture. An unforgettable role.

Even playing with the cast of great actors in the picture, Ronald Reagan was memorable. Those actors included Claude Raines, Betty Field, Judith Anderson, Charles Coburn, Robert Cummings, and Ann Sheridan.

Largely as a result of his arresting performance in the motion picture, Ronald Reagan's agent, at that time Lew Wasserman, was able to triple his salary at Warner's—bringing him in more than $3,000 a week. Like many of the lucky breaks one gets in life, Reagan's came at a time when it did him the least possible amount of good.

It was 1942. He was in the service. The country was at war.

Since 1935, Ronald Reagan had been a reserve second lieutenant with the 14th Cavalry Regiment at Des Moines. He had been accepted despite his eyesight—for a very simple reason.

He had cheated. During the medical examination, he had peeked through fingers held closely together as he placed the cardboard over one eye, so he could vaguely make out the letters on the chart. Squinting through a pinpoint hole in a paper or through fingers closely held together has the effect of allowing a nearsighted person to see distant objects or letters more clearly. It was a simple but effective stratagem to beat the eye test.

Now, of course, with the advent of Pearl Harbor and the declaration of war on two fronts, the country needed everyone it could get to join the armed services. On April 14, 1942, Ronald Reagan was inducted into the United States Army.

The medics were tougher now. When Reagan reported to Fort Dixon in San Francisco, he was immediately disqualified from combat duty. He retained his rank, but was made a liaison officer in charge of loading transports in the harbor.

That didn't last long. The military, which had become woefully inadequate over the years between the end of World War I and the bombing of Pearl Harbor largely because of inaction, was expanding rapidly in many directions, particularly in the direction of air power. There was no Air Force. An "Army Air Corps" was now hastily and dramatically added to the Army. This included fighter pilots, bomber pilots, officers involved in flying planes, ground forces, and support groups of all types.

One of these groups was the First Air Force Motion Picture Unit, assigned to produce documentaries and training films for the pilots and crewmen who would be manning the ships. It was, in effect, a propaganda unit, and because it would be involved in making films and other types of visual aids, it was situated in Culver City, at the old Hal Roach Studio. Ronald Reagan went to war only ten miles from Warner Brothers!

It was to this unit that he was assigned after those few desultory weeks in San Francisco. In fact, he found that he could live at home in Beverly Hills; it was as if he had never entered the service. Like most of the actors involved in the First Air Force Motion Picture Unit, he was somewhat bitter about the work.

Dubbed the "Culver City Commandos" by real soldiers, these officers were understandably bitter. The Hal Roach Studio was even nicknamed "Fort Wacky." Reagan was made personnel officer of the unit and—largely because of his excellent voice and diction—assigned to be narrator for all training films.

He was given a part in the film *This Is the Army*, a propaganda picture made to build morale on the home front. Later he was narrator for *Target Tokyo*, a training film made to prepare the pilots of B-29 Superfortresses for the firebombing raids on Japan.

He worked on a special training film rushed into production when it was discovered that American P-40 fighters were shooting down their own planes instead of the Japanese Zeros they were after. Investigation showed that the two planes looked practically alike at a distance of a thousand yards.

A Zero was captured and taken to San Diego, where it was flown side by side with a P-40. Film crews shot pictures of the planes from all angles, demonstrating exactly how a pilot could tell them apart. The prints were rushed to the South Pacific to clear up the confusion.

But much of the work at the First Air Force Motion Picture Unit was run-of-the-mill guff. The Hollywood actors involved in the military gamesmanship of the unit chafed at the restrictions and the odd orders that sometimes came through. One hotshot who came in from Washington had the bright idea to give the Hollywood soldiers—officers and enlisted men—close-order drill, and finally marched them four abreast across the company lot to the flagpole. Reagan, by then a captain, shouted out: "Splendid body of men. With half this many, I could conquer MGM."

In one gag film made by the crew to alleviate boredom, Reagan played a general, with a huge cigar in his mouth, briefing a bomber squadron. When the map rolled up, the pin-up of a pretty girl appeared on the wall.

On December 9, 1945, Captain Ronald Reagan received his

discharge from the Army. He returned immediately to Warner Brothers to resume his contract.

Things were simply not the same anymore. The business had changed. Not only were there new actors and actresses around, but there was a new public out there, too. Ronald Reagan was quite aware of the fact that not many of the people who walked into motion-picture theaters even knew what he looked like now.

There were rifts in his marriage, too. Things were not going smoothly at all. News leaked out to the columnists that all was not well.

As an actor, Ronald Reagan knew that he had his work cut out for him. He had to remind the public that he had been a star. He had to find the right film to make his comeback in.

As a married man, he had his work cut out for him. But he did not know exactly what to do.

His main problem was to get a blockbuster of a picture to star in. It was not an easy thing to do at all. One of the scripts he liked particularly well was called *Stallion Road*. It dealt with horse ranching and would be shot on location. Ronald Reagan liked the idea of that. It was also to be one of the first Technicolor pictures to be made after the war. Humphrey Bogart and Lauren Bacall would be starring in it; they were top box-office draws at the time.

However, the Bogarts almost immediately decided the picture was not for them, and Zachary Scott and Alexis Smith were brought in to do it. The budget was slashed and the Technicolor was downgraded to plain old black and white.

The movie was not a rousing success. But Ronald Reagan always liked it because it introduced him to horse-breeding. During the filming of the picture, he hired a former Italian cavalry officer, Nino Pepitone, as his coach. Later on, Pepitone helped him set up his own horse ranch—first in the San Fernando Valley, where he owned a small ranch with his first wife, and later on in the more distant Malibu Hills, and finally in the big spread he bought in the Santa Ynez Mountains.

At the time, postwar Hollywood was in a mess. Labor conditions in the movies were chaotic. They always had been, but during the war the American Federation of Labor had given the country a no-strike pledge "for the duration." Now the war was over, and strikes were occurring everywhere in the industry. There were demands for higher salaries, better working conditions. But there was also evidence of big political moves, including the fear of a takeover by the Communists.

In the 1930s, many intellectuals, in Hollywood as elsewhere, had turned to Marxism as the only alternative to a collapsing capitalist system. With the Russians allies during the war, Communism had become almost an "in" thing—at least a chic and defensible ideology.

But with the end of hostilities people in the industry began polarizing to either the left or the right. Ronald Reagan became an officer of the Screen Actors Guild and held a position on the board of directors in 1938. He turned out to be quite a good negotiator and bargainer. In effect he was a good solid "union man" who was able to get the union what it wanted.

He joined the American Veterans Committee and the Hollywood Independent Citizens Committee of Arts, Sciences and Professions. Some of these organizations supported leftist causes, which made him uncomfortable. He began to seek some way of ascertaining who the Communists were and then of trying to root them out.

In 1947, he appeared as a witness before the House Committee on Un-American Activities in its investigation of Communism in the film industry. The same year he was elected president of the Screen Actors Guild. Two years later he was made chairman of the Motion Picture Industry Council, representing labor, management, and other factions. It was becoming a widely accepted fact that he was a skilled arbitrator.

Although his talents were leading him somewhat away from the picture business, he continued to make movies, trying to regain some of his star status. He did a good job in John van Druten's stage hit *The Voice of the Turtle* in 1947, and even received accolades from the critics. Later he played in a Norman Krasna farce, *John Loves Mary*, and then he made *The Girl from Jones Beach.*

His best role during that period was his appearance in *The Hasty Heart*, an adaptation of John Patrick's big Broadway hit. But he was beginning to chafe at the bit. His marriage was on the rocks. A divorce was in the offing. He was making good money, but he was beginning to feel unfulfilled. His life needed a new direction.

He was cast opposite Ida Lupino in a picture to be titled *Fugitive from Terror*. However, on June 19 he broke his leg in six places while playing in a charity baseball game and had to withdraw from the film. It was at just about this time that his divorce from Jane Wyman became final.

Ronald Reagan was not a happy man.

5

Life in a Fairy Tale

It all began for Anne Frances Robbins in a way almost diametrically opposite to the way it had begun for Ronald Reagan. While he had emotional and psychological security in a close-knit, loving family, he grew up in an economic atmosphere in which there was almost constantly a problem of finding enough money to live on from one day to the next.

As for "Anne"—almost from the day of her birth her mother thought of her as Nancy, not Anne—she had economic security from the beginning, but did not have emotional or psychological security until later on in her life. Her mother and father, who had married some four years before her birth on July 6, 1921, were at that point pursuing divergent paths.

Her mother was a professional actress, working in the theater under her maiden name, Edith Luckett. Her father, Kenneth Robbins, was not interested in the theater at all. Robbins was solidly middle-class. His family had lived in New England for generations. His father owned a prosperous business. A Princeton graduate, Robbins was a friend of many other rather "comfortable" people around the metropolitan area.

Edith Luckett and Kenneth Robbins had fallen in love while Robbins was still in uniform, after having volunteered for duty in World War I. They were married before he left for overseas, and Edith continued acting while he served out his time. When he returned she gave it all up to be with him. But it soon became obvious that some aspects of their relationship had been altered irrevocably.

Kenneth Robbins's father owned a flourishing woolen mill

in Pittsfield, Massachusetts, the New England town where Kenneth was born, and he had worked there for his father for a number of years. When he left home he had purchased an automobile franchise in New Jersey, and upon his return from the service he continued selling cars in the prosperous years that followed the war. For a short time he and Edith lived in New Jersey, and it was during this period that Anne Frances was born in a New York hospital.

Shortly after Nancy's birth, the differences that were plaguing the young couple's marriage became too pronounced to ignore, and they split up. Edith Luckett went back to the stage, taking her daughter with her.

Edith had become interested in the theater through the influence of her uncle, Joseph L. Luckett. Luckett at one time was manager of the Columbia Theater in Washington, D.C., where he had presented plays with various stock companies featuring such popular actors as John Mason, John Drew, and Lillian Russell.

It was through her uncle—always "Uncle Joe" to Edith—that she got her start in show business. Chauncey Alcott, a popular songwriter and singer of the era—he wrote "My Wild Irish Rose" and "When Irish Eyes Are Smiling"—was touring the country singing concerts composed of his own songs and other favorites of the time. His accompanist while on tour was his sister at the piano.

Alcott was scheduled to sing in Washington one night when his sister became ill. Edith Luckett applied for the job. Although she was not an accomplished pianist, she managed to practice all Alcott's repertoire, and once on stage, gave a credible imitation of a professional accompanist. From that moment on, she was in "show business."

Eventually she got jobs with many of the great actors and actresses of her day, including David Belasco, George M. Cohan, Walter Huston, Louis Calhern, ZaSu Pitts, and Spencer Tracy. One of her favorites and a close friend was Alla Nazimova. Edith—called Dee Dee by her show-business acquaintances—had begun her career playing a small part in an

Alla Nazimova production. When her daughter was born, Edith selected Nazimova as the baby's godmother.

Now that with the departure of her husband she was on her own, Edith Luckett made the rounds of the Broadway theater, tried out for a few new roles, and settled down into a stage career again. In those days not all the legitimate theater was located in New York. Working in the theater demanded a great deal of travel. An actor or an actress had to go from one town and city to another, spending months on the road as a member of the "troupe"—the company of actors and actresses that took a popular show to dozens of out-of-the-way places that otherwise would see no legitimate theater at all.

Being moved about from hotel to hotel was unsettling for young Nancy, and for Edith herself. After a few months of it she realized she was not up to it any more than her daughter was. She decided that she might be doing irreparable harm to her child by subjecting her to the nomadic life necessary to a professional in the theater.

For help, Edith turned to one of her sisters. The Luckett family was a large one; Edith was one of nine siblings. Her sister Virginia had married Audley Galbraith, and the Galbraiths lived with their daughter, Charlotte, in Bethesda, Maryland. Virginia invited Edith to leave Nancy with the Galbraiths so that Virginia could take care of Nancy as one of the family. Reluctantly, but thankfully, Edith accepted her sister's offer. And so when Nancy was two years old, she settled down with the Galbraiths in Bethesda. In that way, Edith felt that Nancy could get as normal an upbringing as was possible under the circumstances. Whenever Edith's travels brought her back to New York, her sister would take Nancy down to the city to visit her mother backstage and in the residential hotels and brownstone apartments the theatrical crowd lived in. From her earliest childhood, Nancy grew up under the mesmerizing spell of grease paint and the glamour of theatrical life.

It was not always an easy life. Nancy and her cousin Charlotte lived the typical happy-go-lucky life of kids during the

1920s—but there were gaps; there were details missing. It was her mother whom Nancy missed the most. She looked forward eagerly to seeing her whenever she could get to the city on those visits to the Broadway scene.

Later on she once said:

"It is hard for me to understand children who can't wait to get away from home. I missed my mother so, and I was so happy when I could be with her."

And indeed when she was with her, there was nothing like it. She would put on her mother's makeup, dress up in her stage clothes, and strut around pretending she was an actress. She would go down to the theater and see the shows her mother was in over and over, watching the audience react from the wings, and sometimes even sitting out front with the spectators.

Even in Bethesda, Nancy was always play-acting. She talked her mother into buying her a blond wig so that she would look more like Mary Pickford—the actress everyone was talking about at the time. She went around for weeks under false blond hair, pretending she was the great motion-picture star.

She saw her father infrequently, although she kept in touch with him even after he remarried. She visited him occasionally in the New Jersey apartment where he and his second wife lived. Such visits were not always totally successful.

Nancy liked her father's new wife, a pleasant woman who tried to make things comfortable for her, but she seemed to have a difficult time getting along with her father. For one thing, she resented the fact that he had left her mother, and for another, she was tempted to blame him for whatever had gone wrong between the two of them.

One time she was arguing with her father and he made an unpleasant remark about her mother that Nancy felt was unfair, and she told him so. He was not used to being contradicted, and he lost his temper. To punish her, he locked her up in the bathroom.

It was a traumatic experience for Nancy. She had never been

treated that way before. She felt trapped in a psychological as well as physical way when she found that she could not get out. The incident was engraved indelibly on her memory.

To her father's credit, he immediately realized that he had overreacted. He unlocked the door and tried to soothe Nancy until she stopped crying. Yet even though her father apologized profusely when he realized how affected she was by the incident, she never really forgave him.

One day in 1929 her mother came to see her in Bethesda and took her out on the screened porch of the house to talk to her privately. She told Nancy that she had met a man—a surgeon, named Loyal Davis—on a boat trip and that he had asked her to marry him. She did not know how Nancy would feel about it. That was what she wanted to find out.

"If you don't want me to marry him, I won't," Edith told Nancy. "I know it's a difficult question to put to you, but I must do it."

Nancy asked her mother if she wanted to marry Dr. Davis.

"Yes, Nancy, I do," her mother said, hugging her. "I wouldn't have mentioned him to you if I didn't."

Nancy thought a bit and then said: "Are you going to keep on acting?"

"No, darling. I've decided that if I marry him I'll give it up and live in Chicago with him."

"And what about me?" Nancy asked.

"You'll live there with us. I thought you understood that!"

Nancy's face lit up. "I'll be glad if you marry him then, and I'll be happy to live with you."

That was all there was to it. Edith Luckett finished her tour with the company of *Elmer the Great* in Chicago, then sent for Nancy. Nancy rode on the train to Chicago with her Aunt Virginia and met her mother at the station. Edith introduced the stranger with her as Dr. Loyal Davis, her husband-to-be.

Nancy thought the tall, considerate man was all right, but she did not warm up to him immediately. It was simply not her way to go overboard in an emotional way on a moment's notice. On his side, the surgeon was a reserved man himself. He already had a young son, Richard, about Nancy's age, by his first wife. Richard was living away from him with his mother.

Nancy acted as flower girl at the wedding, held in May 1929, at the Fourth Presbyterian Church in Chicago.

It took time for Nancy to get to know her stepfather. He was a hardworking surgeon and spent a great deal of time on rounds at the hospital. In fact, he was a very important man in medical circles.

Loyal Davis had grown up in Galesburg, Illinois, and as a young man had wanted to be a railroad engineer like his father. However, in his formative years he had been befriended by a doctor in town and had become interested in a medical career. Because his family had little money, he was obliged to work his way through college and medical school, but he did so without trouble. He studied at Knox College and Northwestern University.

He served his residency at Cook County Hospital in Chicago, and then spent time working with important surgeons such as Harvey Cushing in Boston, and others around the country. Cushing, of course, was the father of neurosurgery in America, and working with him had such an impact on Loyal Davis that he decided to concentrate on surgery himself. He became associate in surgery at Peter Bent Brigham Hospital in Boston, and when he returned to Chicago he became the first full-time brain surgeon in the city.

Later on he served as chief of surgery at Passavant Northwestern University Memorial Hospital in Chicago. During World War I he served as a medical officer.

The marriage was a good one from the start. Dr. Davis was not an outgoing or social person, but Edith was. She soon brought him out of his shell, and helped enhance his professional standing by improving his social contacts. She was a woman who had always attracted people to her.

As for Nancy, her relationship with her stepfather had moments of unease and difficulty during the first weeks and months. However, she soon found that this man was a sensitive and kindly person. Because he was already a father, he seemed to understand the feelings of his stepdaughter and knew how to treat them—mostly with compassion, with understanding, and with love. It seemed to work. He did all he could to counteract any communications gap that might exist between them.

Within a reasonable span of time, Nancy found that her new father had become what she had always thought a father should be—and she took to him completely.

In Bethesda, Nancy had always gone to public school, but in Chicago her new father enrolled her in Girls' Latin School. His son, Richard, her stepbrother, was enrolled in Boys' Latin School, and it was only natural that Nancy should go to the sister school.

Several years after Nancy joined the Davis family, Richard's mother, with whom he was living, died, and Richard moved in with the rest of them. They lived in an apartment overlooking Lake Shore Drive and Lake Michigan, in a building near the Drake Hotel. Nancy could walk to school along the lake most of the year, except when the wind was too cold and the waves crashed against the concrete walls.

Girls' Latin School was harder than public school, but Nancy was quite good at her studies. Still, she enjoyed extracurricular activities much more. Even at that time she had decided to follow in the footsteps of her mother and take up a career in the theater. She was able to join the Dramatic Club and acted in some of the plays.

After she had been in Chicago five years, she knew that she had finally found her real life. She was with her mother all the time, and she liked her stepfather, who acted more like a father than her own father had. When Loyal Davis told Nancy that he wanted to make her officially his daughter, she was pleased, but she was also somewhat worried about what her own father might think.

There was a law on the books at the time permitting a child fourteen years old or older to choose whether to have a natural parent or a stepparent as the legal parent. And so when Nancy was fourteen, she decided that she would become Loyal Davis's legal daughter. That meant she would change her name from Anne Frances Robbins to Nancy Davis. To do so, Nancy was required by law to get her natural father's permission to make the change.

She was still in touch with him—and especially with his mother, her grandmother, who had always considered her only granddaughter a favorite. And so she made the difficult journey to New Jersey to tell her father what she wanted.

When she showed him the papers, he read them through silently, then looked up at her.

"Is this what you want?"

"Yes," she told him.

Later, she wrote in her autobiography:

"He signed them, although I'm sure it hurt him to do so. I know it hurt his mother, but it was what I wanted."

And so Anne Frances Robbins became Nancy Davis.

During her high school years, Nancy spent her summers with her family, sometimes visiting California friends like the Walter Hustons, the Spencer Tracys, Louis Calhern, ZaSu Pitts, and others in show business who had worked with Dee Dee Luckett in her many years on the stage.

Nancy's life was an exciting one for someone enchanted with the theater. During a vacation with the Walter Hustons at their cabin at Lake Arrowhead, Nancy met Josh Logan, a producer who was making his name at the time, and a young actor in Hollywood named Jimmy Stewart. She also knew Walter Huston's sister, Margaret Jones, married to the scenic designer Robert Edmond Jones.

It was Josh Logan who persuaded Walter Huston to take on the role of Peter Stuyvesant in *Knickerbocker Holiday*, which turned out to be the actor's most memorable role on Broadway.

Nancy herself was making good in acting at Girls' Latin School. She had played in a number of dramatic presentations, but one of her best—and most prophetic—was that of the leading lady in the senior class play. The play was titled *First Lady*!

A clipping from the 1939 yearbook described Nancy's dedication to the dramatic arts:

"The cast has straggled in for rehearsal. In one corner two or three girls are trying desperately to learn their lines, but in the other corner Nancy, with by far the longest role, is perched gaily on top of the radiator, apparently telling a grand story. . . . When the fatal night comes, Nancy knows not only her own lines but everybody else's. She picks up the cue her terrified classmates forget to give, improvises speeches for all and sundry. Just a part of the game for Nancy."

One of her lines spoken in the play foreshadowed the women's liberation movement by some years:

"They ought to elect the First Lady and then let her husband be President."

After her graduation from Girls' Latin School in 1939, Nancy opted to go to Smith College, in Northampton, Massachusetts. Because it was so far away from home, she decided she would go for only two years, then come home to live in Chicago.

However, as it happened, she stayed the full four years and graduated in 1943. A great many things occurred between her freshman year and her graduation. And during those important four years, Nancy Davis changed from a teenager to a mature young woman. She also decided definitely on a career in the theater.

Not only did she change emotionally and intellectually, but physically as well. During her first year in college, she was a chunky, laughing, devil-may-care person. By the time she graduated, she was slimmer, more reserved, and much, much quieter.

During those important years, Nancy made her debut in Chicago at a tea dance held at the Casino Club in January 1940, just after she had entered Smith. It so happened that the Princeton Triangle Club was in town, and every member had been invited to her debut. Nancy had met several men from Princeton at Smith and was interested especially in one named Frank Birney.

He attended her party, and she spent much of her time with him there. Then when she returned to campus in the fall, she saw him again and again whenever there was a college affair to which men were invited.

Nancy would also go down to New Jersey to the Princeton football games with several of her friends. At other times she would invite Frank Birney to come to Smith for the dances. Occasionally they met in New York—under the clock at the Biltmore—for dates and shows. These were memorable weekends for Nancy. She was living the life of the Beautiful People before there were Beautiful People.

However, she was finding it somewhat difficult to get her studies under control. Never a "bright" student, she had to work hard, but once she had her studies in hand and had learned how to take tests, she began to do more work in the campus theater. She was involved in both dramatic shows and in musicals.

In the winter of 1941, when Nancy was a junior, a group of her friends were writing and acting in a musical comedy, a loosely constructed production that was not much more than a bunch of songs tied together without a real story line. Nancy had little to do with the writing, but she was cast as the lead.

Called *Banderlog*, it was the first musical that had ever been done at Smith. It turned out to be a hit. As the lead, Nancy received a big hand when she finished one of her main numbers. The show was a definite success, and Nancy felt that her role in it was her triumphant send-off in show business.

This euphoria was to be short-lived. The next day, Nancy and the rest of the cast were enjoying themselves at a coffee shop near the campus when someone happened by and mentioned that the Japanese had just bombed Pearl Harbor. No one really took that seriously; there were war scares all the time in 1941, with Europe in the midst of a battle to the death with Adolf Hitler.

Nevertheless, Nancy immediately realized that the country was at war. It was obvious almost at once that no one's life was going to continue on in the same comfortable fashion as before. One of the most worried was Frank Birney. He had been having a great deal of trouble with his grades and was afraid he might flunk out. He was also worried about the war. Nancy and he talked about it, but nothing seemed clear to either of them at the time. Everyone around them was as confused as they were.

On December 13—a Saturday, one day short of a week after the bombing of Pearl Harbor—Frank's body was discovered on the railroad tracks near the Princeton station. He had apparently fallen in front of a train while trying to cross the tracks. He had been on his way to New York to meet his half sister. No one really knew what had happened, and there could be only speculation about the details.

It was a devastating experience for Nancy. She confessed later in her autobiography that she did not really know if she had been in love with Frank Birney or not, or whether the two of them would ever have married, but she recalled that it took her "a long time" to get over his death.

"I felt a deep loss then and a little scar still remains inside, but I learned that life goes on and you go on with it. I got back into college activities and eventually began to date again."

She also continued with her acting. During her college summers she always stayed in the Berkshires and worked in the stock companies that dotted the New England area. It was there, as well as at college, that she learned the theater from the bottom up. Typical of the way summer stock functioned, she would be building and painting scenery one minute, mending and ironing costumes the next, delivering messages from one person to another, and then sweeping the stage clean for the night's performance. At the same time she would be rehearsing her lines for her appearance the next week. And in her spare time, she might be going down to the village to pin up posters for the show on the streetlamps and telephone poles.

The year 1943 was not a propitious year for a young unmarried woman to graduate from college. The war was still on, and would be for another two years. There were almost no men around—and those that were around were engaged in important business that did not leave them too much time to play around or date interested young women.

Nancy's father had joined the armed services for his second stint in uniform and was overseas. Nancy's mother was living alone and did not need the large apartment. She sublet it and moved into the Drake Hotel. Nancy joined her there to wait for the war to end and Loyal Davis to come home.

Nancy decided that she would study to be a nurse's aide—it seemed a patriotic thing to do at the time—and in her extra time she got a job working in the college shop at Marshall Field's, the largest department store around.

Loyal Davis returned before the war ended. The Davises moved from the Drake Hotel back into their old apartment. Nancy's father had returned early because he was ill; he eventually recovered.

It was at this point that one of her mother's oldest and dearest friends, ZaSu Pitts, telephoned from New York to tell Nancy that she was in the touring cast of a play titled *Ramshackle Inn* and that there was a part available for her.

Although Nancy suspected that her mother had had a great deal to do with the "sudden part," she seized the opportunity and went to New York immediately. She got the part. She also moved in with ZaSu Pitts, who was missing her own daughter, Ann, very much at the time.

It wasn't much of a part, as parts go, but she was acting on the stage! "I think I had one line," she recalled later. "I was a girl who was kidnapped and who was up in the attic most of the time—until I broke loose, came down the stairs, delivered my one line, and they took me away."

Nancy traveled across the country with the play and wound up doing the "subway circuit" in New York, playing theaters in Brooklyn, Long Island, the Bronx, and Manhattan. "You performed seven nights a week with matinees on Saturday and Sunday. It was hard work."

She stayed in New York after the play folded and made the rounds trying to get new parts. In fact, it was ZaSu once again who helped her get a part in another of her own plays. This one was *Cordelia*, and in it Nancy played in Boston, Hartford, and several other New England cities.

Once again she wound up in New York, making the rounds of the theatrical casting offices. Spencer Tracy was cast in a play titled *The Rugged Path*, and as a friend of the family, he invited her to watch rehearsals. He also figured in one of Nancy's most exciting episodes in New York.

Tracy's friend and MGM colleague Clark Gable was in town, and Tracy suggested to Gable that he take Nancy Davis out rather than visit the night spots unescorted. And so Gable took Nancy to the World Series games in town, and later to restaurants and nightclubs everywhere. It was very exciting for Nancy and was over only too soon when Gable's stay in New York ended and he went back to Hollywood and work.

It was 1946, and Broadway was having a smash year. Nancy finally read for a part in a new play Michael Myerberg was producing. And when it was all over, she got the part! The show was *Lute Song*, a musical starring Mary Martin and Yul Brynner—and Nancy was cast as an oriental, Tsi Chun, who was lady-in-waiting to the character played by Mary Martin.

The show opened in New Haven and Boston before going to New York, and then once there it played about six months. Nancy Davis even got a good review herself. In New York, the show played at the Plymouth Theater. When it closed, Mary Martin left the cast. Nancy Davis was invited to go on the road with the show, but decided against it and took a new part with ZaSu Pitts in *Cordelia*, which was in tryouts out of town.

The show never made it to Broadway, but Nancy got a job on the road in a George Abbott production of *The Late Christopher Bean*, which even played Chicago, where her parents and friends could see her.

Back in New York there were parts, but Nancy didn't seem to get any of them. She did play in several television productions, one of them a TV version of her first show, *Ramshackle Inn*. Then she did another one called *Broken Dishes*.

Someone at the television studio made a kinescope of *Ramshackle Inn*—in those days there wasn't any such thing as videotape—and sent it out to the West Coast. Someone at

Metro-Goldwyn-Mayer saw the show and made a call to Nancy's agent.

Meanwhile, Nancy called her mother in Chicago, who called Spencer Tracy in Hollywood, who called director George Cukor, arranging to have him make the test of Nancy. By the time Nancy got to the Coast, it was arranged that she should make the test with Howard Keel, who had just been signed on at MGM.

She never saw the test. But someone else apparently did—and liked it. Nancy was given the standard studio contract, then pegged at $250 a week to start. That was the year 1949—a year that was going to turn out to be one of the most momentous in Nancy Davis's life.

It was the year she met Ronald Reagan.

6

The Courtship

If Ronald Reagan had met Nancy Davis in one of the motion pictures of the era in which he might have appeared, he would immediately have realized he was in love with her and would have pursued her as the hero of any story should.

If Nancy Davis had met Ronald Reagan in one of the motion pictures of the era in which she might have been cast, she would immediately have known she loved him and would have done almost anything humanly possible to attract him and try to make him fall in love with her.

But real life was not a movie scenario, even in 1949.

Ronald Reagan considered himself a failed husband, a man whose wife had left him and whose children were available to him only on weekends. In spite of his cheerful ways and his optimistic, upbeat disposition, he had been crushed by the collapse of his marriage and simply did not want to think about a new romantic relationship at all. His attitude paralleled the fictional attitude of the solitary, anti-woman, rugged male hero of the action-adventure motion pictures of the time.

Nancy Davis was still looking for someone with whom she could form a romantic attachment. From the beginning of her life, she had been placed in a negative position by men—first of all and most excruciatingly by her own father when he left her and her mother. Although she had succeeded in replacing him in her mind and in her heart with her stepfather, Dr. Loyal Davis, scars remained on her psyche from the initial trauma of what she considered her father's rejection of her and her mother. In addition to those unpleasant truths, she had experienced another painful ending to an attachment when Frank Birney had died. From that time on, her relationships with men had been superficial and somewhat tenuous.

And yet in spite of what had happened to her, she continued to entertain hopes. Now those hopes had been revived by her meeting with Ronald Reagan, the final realization of a fantasy encounter she might have imagined back in her college days when she had seen him on the movie screen of one of the theaters near the Smith campus.

In spite of the personality difficulties that stood in the way of a quick, happy, and healthy romance, there were other factors that were moving these two people closer and closer together. Both were now at critical points of their lives when they were more or less marking time in their own loneliness, simultaneously reaching out for someone or something to touch—a new turning in their existence, a new friendship, a new outlook on life.

More than a simple broken marriage troubled Ronald Reagan. He was almost forty years old—a mature man whose career was beginning to founder. He had been blessed with good luck when he started at Warner Brothers, and he had almost attained permanent stardom upon completion of his memorable role in *King's Row*, but his luck had deserted him at almost the magic moment of attainment. The bombing of Pearl Harbor and his years of military service had denied him the necessary exposure to his public and had doomed him to a long period of obscurity.

Now, when he tried to find parts in pictures that would bolster his image, he found that he was just one more forgotten man, with a whole new breed of actors pushing up and shoving the old ones aside. Besides, his natural interest in politics had not helped him one bit. In fact, it had definitely worked against him. The studio bosses who usually sat across the conference table from him during negotiations between the Screen Actors Guild and the producers were the ones who decided who got the good roles and profitable contracts in a business that was beginning to struggle for survival for the first time since the advent of sound some two decades before.

He was in trouble, and he knew it. He needed a big role in an impressive and successful motion picture. It was the only thing that could possibly get him back in the limelight again. Times were changing; movie heroes were not the same in the postwar world as they had been before. To be successful an actor had to insist on being cast only in roles that made sense to the public. Ronald Reagan's ideas about good roles did not always parallel the ideas of the studio bosses.

Nancy Davis was also facing a career crisis every bit as formidable as Ronald Reagan's. She was twenty-eight years old. Most women her age were married or were involved in successful careers of a permanent nature. Nancy was, like Ronald Reagan, in a kind of limbo caused by the peculiar demands of their profession. In her case, the limbo was not self-created, but was imposed by the studio system of which she was an integral part.

On Nancy's side, she was intrigued by Ronald Reagan, for she had never known anyone quite so honest and open in his opinions and points of view, or so eager to talk about them at such great length. Reticence was ingrained in Nancy; although her mother was chatty and outgoing in the same manner as Ronald Reagan, her father—Loyal Davis—was quiet, rather stern, and forbidding in aspect at times. She liked the genial bonhomie that radiated from Ronald Reagan wherever he went. She tended to bask in it, as she might bask in the heat of the warm California sun. From the moment she met him and became acquainted with him, she always called him Ronnie, and never Dutch, or Ron, as others did.

On Ronnie's part, he was fascinated by Nancy and overwhelmed by her interest in what he might be saying. He had always talked too much. He knew that, and he had always tried to curb the tendency to outlast everyone else subjected to his marathon monologues. But he saw that the longer he talked, the more interested Nancy was in what he was saying. Or at least she *appeared* to be—which was really the most important thing anyway.

Yet Ronnie and Nancy did not in any surface manner communicate these important facts to each other in their first meetings. Each considered the other an interesting specimen inhabiting the same part of the Hollywood zoo. It was *inside* them—in the privacy of their own psyches—that the two understood completely that they were absolutely and irrevocably meant for each other. Unfortunately, these elements of their personalities were screened from each other by their own inhibitions, anxieties, and concerns.

Each was a born homebody—an individual who loved to spend a quiet evening at home, or in the home of a close friend. Each loved the quiet life and ability to recharge personal energies in solitude—or the nearest thing to solitude.

Although Nancy was born in New York and Ronnie in Illinois, each loved Southern California, not only for the ease of its life, but for the wide-open expansiveness of the countryside and the lush preserves of ancient woods and forests that were there for their enjoyment. In spite of Nancy's longtime residence in the rather posh surrounding of Dr. Loyal Davis's expensive Lake Shore apartment suite and in spite of Ronnie's need for people around him to listen to his conversation, they both loved to be together in the marvelous paradise that was outdoor Southern California.

Because they were the special people they were, they did not play the game of romance in its most typical and theatrically recognizable form. If anything, their relationship resembled an underground romance rather than one that existed out in the open, above the ground as it were.

Ronnie played it in much the same manner as he had played it during the first days of his separation from Jane Wyman. He dropped in at Dave Chasen's quiet restaurant in Beverly Hills one or two times a week; he liked to sit on a comfortable banquette with paperwork from the Screen Actors Guild spread out in front of him on the table.

He continued to date other women on the Hollywood scene

sporadically. His closest friends guessed what was going on in his mind; in fact, they knew more about what Ronnie was up to than Ronnie did himself. The disintegration and ruin of his marriage had affected Ronnie a great deal more than he realized. Although he understood his own moodiness and his own desire to avoid thinking about what had happened, he did not really comprehend the total devastation it had visited on his own ego.

A thin-skinned individual who always presented a sunny and optimistic face to the world, Ronnie was tormented by pain and remorse. Not only was his first wife's rejection bothering him, but the fact that his career was sinking added to his psychological burden. He was carrying a great weight, but he was determined that no one should know about it.

In his youth Ronnie had developed a very simple ploy to keep his hurt from showing and to overcome pain. His weapon was humor. In their boyhood, both he and his brother, Moon, had practiced one-liners, jokes, and wisecracks to turn away insults, or attacks of one kind or another, or anything else that might hurt them.

By now Ronnie was skilled at one-line ripostes. He used them often in his union negotiations. Even during his days in the service at Fort Hal Roach he had honed this practice almost to perfection. He had always subscribed to *Reader's Digest,* and on the day of its delivery, he would speed-read it from cover to cover during the evening, memorizing the jokes and repeating them to the awe and amazement of his colleagues working with him in the special screen unit.

And now, in his loneliness and depression—a depression he did not really allow anyone else to see—he continued to use these humorous sallies to ward off things that might hurt him.

In turn, his inability to reason out his own aversion to involvement with a woman—caused by his own fear of being hurt again—screened the truth about his feelings for Nancy. He simply took her for granted as one other person he could safely date. He turned a casual face to the world and surrounded himself with people from all parts of the Hollywood scene; he deliberately did not concentrate on any one of them in any way.

It kept the columnists guessing. And, in a way, it kept Ronnie himself from seeing too clearly what was happening in his own heart. Nancy had a hold on it; he was not totally unaware of her hold, but he resisted letting himself know how he really felt about it.

As for Nancy, she pretty well knew she had met the man she wanted. But she understood this complex man's problems probably better than he did. She empathized with his hurt and his distrust of women in a romantic sense. She simply played along with him, accepting every chance he offered to be with him.

Sometimes he would take her with him to Dave Chasen's restaurant, where they would have a quiet dinner before taking a ride along the Pacific Highway to observe the late sunset, or the moon hovering in the sky above them.

They were usually alone, although at times they might visit mutual friends. It was a very quiet romance, one that was almost a nonromance. Ronnie's friends never guessed which woman he actually preferred out of the dozens he dated.

Sidney Skolsky noticed him out with someone he was not familiar with in December, and wrote in his column that Ronnie was "going with Nancy Davis," and then, not really knowing who she was, he described her as "a pretty model." Immediately the columnist linked the Reagan name with Monica Lewis, Adele Gergens, and Patricia Neal—all actresses—and even with Jane Wyman.

"His idea of a date is to take Nancy, Monica, or Pat to a restaurant for dinner. This takes hours, for he talks and talks. Occasionally he likes to go dancing."

Because their relationship was so astonishingly low-profile, another columnist called it "a romance of a couple who have no vices." And he went on to write:

"Not for them the hothouse atmosphere of nightclubs, the smoky little rooms and the smell of Scotch. They eat at Dave Chasen's, they spend their evenings in the homes of friends, they drive along the coast and look at the sea and a lot of times they're quiet. They go as 'steady,' according to one reporter, as any couple in Hollywood and Nancy knits Reagan argyle socks, though she doesn't cook for him."

And so it was that during the winter of 1949 and all through 1950 and 1951 and into 1952 they continued to see each other. It was never a sudden flash of "romance" that Hollywood gossips and screenwriters wrote about, but a more prolonged, deeply rooted, and slowly blossoming relationship that was developing.

Nancy continued with her career. She got a starring role in a rather unorthodox motion picture titled *The Next Voice You Hear,* one of those fantasies dreamed up by Hollywood scriptwriters trying to invent a striking plot twist. In it, God kept interrupting radio programs in order to warn the populace at large that the human race had better shape up or prepare for Armageddon.

Nancy traveled to New York to promote the movie. She starred with James Whitmore, and it was the first time she was ever able to look up at a marquee in New York City and see her name in lights. And it was the first time that she had ever been interviewed by columnists from New York papers. She gave all the predictable answers to their questions and admitted that she was a baseball fan from way back, who rooted for the Yanks *and* the Red Sox both, and even used to trade in theater passes for baseball tickets when she was working on the subway circuit in the theater.

She even told a joke about herself. After the kinescope of her small part in *Ramshackle Inn* had been sent to the West Coast, she was in Chicago with her family.

"And one day," she told a columnist, "the phone rang and it was Dore Schary, the big man at MGM. My, I thought, that test must have been sensational. But all he wanted was to talk to Dr. Davis about his back and an operation."

After she finished making *The Next Voice You Hear,* Nancy was cast in *Rain, Rain Go Away,* once again with James

Whitmore, and with Ralph Meeker and Jean Hagen. When the picture was released it was titled *Shadow in the Sky*.

Next came *People in Love*, starring Ray Milland, John Hodiak, and Jean Hagen, with Lewis Stone. It was released as *Night into Morning*. She also had a bit part playing opposite Fredric March in a segment of *It's a Big Country*.

She starred again in *Talk About a Stranger*, playing opposite George Murphy as his wife.

In contrast to Nancy's career, which seemed to be moving along in a somewhat erratic but positive direction, Ronnie's career was going absolutely nowhere. As he himself had predicted, *That Hagen Girl*, in which he had been costarred with a grown-up Shirley Temple, proved to be a disaster at the box office. Before leaving for England to make *The Hasty Heart*, he had secured the rights to a western novel written by Alan Le May called *Ghost Mountain*, in the hope that he would be assigned to it on his return from England.

"I'm going to pick my own pictures," he told columnist Bob Thomas. "I have come to the conclusion that I could do as good a job of picking as the studio has done. . . . At least I could do no worse." In the same interview, he opined that if his movie career collapsed, he could "always go back to being a sports announcer."

Jack L. Warner read the story and dictated a letter of reprimand to Ronald Reagan—a letter that was not mailed, but whose contents were made known to Ronald Reagan by word of mouth. Warner was covering up the fact that he had assigned the starring role in *Ghost Mountain* to Errol Flynn, whose popularity had never waned through the war years, mainly because the actor had continued to appear in pictures, since he was not involved in the armed forces, and his box-office appeal was at its very peak at war's end.

Reagan knew Flynn had been selected for the picture, but he wrote a letter to the studio executives in May 1950, pretending he did not know what Jack L. Warner had done. The letter was spiced with bits of sarcasm and irony that were not at all lost on the top brass at Warner Brothers who read it. Including Jack L. Warner.

"I know that you will recall our discussion some time ago with regard to *That Hagen Girl*," Reagan wrote. "You agreed the script and role were very weak but asked me to do the picture as a personal favor which I gladly did. At that time you encouraged me to bring in a suitable outdoor script which you agreed to buy as a starring vehicle for me. I found such a property in *Ghost Mountain* and the studio purchased it with me, through MCA, acting as go-between to close the deal with the author.

"Of late there have been 'gossip items' indicating that you plan to star someone else in the story. Naturally I put no stock in these rumors—I know you too well to ever think you'd break your word.

"However, I am anxious to know something of production plans—starting date, etc., in order to better schedule my own plans. Frankly I hope it is soon as I have every confidence in this story."

Of course, the letter did little good, but at least it allowed Ronnie to ventilate some of his fury. What he really wanted was to get some good pictures; he didn't care how he did it, but he knew he would not survive in the Hollywood jungle if he did not play the kinds of parts that people wanted to see him in.

George Ward and Bill Meiklejohn were no longer his agents. The Meiklejohn Agency had been purchased by the Music Corporation of America—MCA—with Ward going off to work for the Myron Selznick Agency, and Meiklejohn heading up talent at Paramount Pictures.

Back at MCA, which had Ronnie's contract, he now belonged to Lew Wasserman. Wasserman knew how dissatisfied Ronnie was with his deal at Warner Brothers, and he entered the fray to try to get him some kind of deal in which he could have more input concerning the roles he would play.

What he wound up with was a one-deal-a-year contract for Ronald Reagan with Warner's. Ronnie could make any other deals he wanted with competing studios, as long as he did one for Warner's during the year.

Ronnie had fallen in love with the outdoors when he had made *Stallion Road*, and he wanted to play more mature he-man roles. He made a series of westerns for other studios, and even played in a baseball picture.

His financial deal with Warner's was very good. All he had to do was sign one contract a year, do the job, and then free-lance wherever he could. This gave him much more time to dabble in what had become his major pastime—ranching.

Starting out with his partnership with Nino Pepitone in the eight-acre spread in Northridge in the San Fernando Valley, Ronnie had learned all he could about keeping horses and about breeding them. He loved to spend his time building paddock fences. On the small ranch in Northridge he laid out a quarter-mile track, with all the inner rail posts slanted at the proper angle, with every post hole dug by hand—most of them by Ronnie himself. He had planned and built a model horse nursery on the ranch, too.

In 1951 Ronnie felt it was time to expand. He bought a 350-acre ranch in the rolling hills of Malibu down by the coast in the Santa Monica Mountains. The spread was located near Lake Malibu, the source of the Malibu "River" that emptied out at Malibu proper.

The scenery in the foothills here was absolutely stunning— rolling hills and tiny mottes of scrub oak, blue skies overhead, and the Pacific Ocean in the distance. He knew he had a feel for ranching, or at least he knew that now he loved the idea of ranching, and he fell to it with a will.

He learned how to raise hay. That was no big deal at all— you simply let the wild grass grow, and then mowed it. However, there was, he discovered, an art to it. He built jumps out of timber and stones to use for running his horses. He designed and built paneled fences for the jumps. He worked on fences all the time, spending days and weeks at it, laboring in the healthy sunshine.

He found that working outside kept him in shape and kept him from thinking too deeply about what was troubling him. He loved the life he was leading—even though the pictures he was making were not improving his image any. Somehow it really didn't seem to matter that much anymore.

He drove a green Cadillac convertible at the time, and he would drive up to the ranch with Nancy Davis in the front seat and take her out to look at what he was doing on the acreage. His daughter, Maureen, and son, Michael, visited the place occasionally, usually on weekends.

Nancy loved the outdoors, too, and was delighted by the limitless space of the ranch. She became acquainted with the children, liked them, and kept coming back to the ranch to be with Ronnie. By now Nancy was secretly admitting to herself that she was in love. And she could read Ronnie well enough to guess that he was in love with her even if he was not quite aware of it himself.

There was one obvious path to follow. Yet it was taking so much time. Every chance Ronnie got he was always driving off to the ranch to clear brush, or taking the train somewhere on "important" Screen Actors Guild business, or running around with this or that contract actress, or doing something other than proposing to her.

"The truth is," Ronnie admitted much later, "I did everything wrong, dating [Nancy] off and on, continuing to volunteer for every guild trip to New York—in short, doing everything which could have lost her if Someone up There hadn't been looking after me."

In his guild activities, Ronnie was working very closely with Bill Holden, whom he had met at the guild and with whom he had attended many meetings and functions. Holden was married to Brenda Marshall, the actress, whose real offstage name was Ardis Ankerson. Holden, Ardis, Ronnie, and Nancy became fast friends during the months of 1950 and 1951. On many of Ronnie's dates with Nancy, the two of them would wind up with the Holdens in their home in the Toluca Lake section of the Valley. The four of them truly enjoyed one another.

Nancy knew what was happening long before Ronnie understood it. She was content to be patient—one who never lost her cool or allowed herself to lose her way. She was waiting for Ronnie to realize that he was in love with her.

"Someplace along here I know there should be a scene of sudden realization," Ronnie wrote later, "the kind we'd write if we were putting this on film. It just didn't happen that way."

No, it did not happen that way at all. But the way it did happen was almost as dramatic and surprising as a motion-picture script might have been.

Ronnie and Holden were acting as guild representatives during a meeting of the Motion Picture Industry Council. They were sitting with dozens of others around a huge round table in the Producers Association meeting room.

There was a lot of talk, the usual give-and-take, but Ronnie suddenly realized that he was paying no attention to what was going on around him, and was, in his own words, "strangely indifferent" to the details of the conversation. He scrawled a note on a scratch pad at his elbow and shoved the paper across the table to Holden.

"To hell with this, how would you like to be best man when I marry Nancy?"

Holden grinned, slapped him on the back, and rose. "It's about time!"

The two of them moved quickly, stalking out of the meeting, leaving the rest of the representatives somewhat disconcerted and imagining all sorts of dire complications in guild relationships that might be coming up in the future. It was some time before they realized that the guild men's departure had nothing to do with business.

While it took Ronnie years to find out where he stood in relation to Nancy Davis, it did not take Nancy Davis that long to find out where Ronald Reagan stood in her mind and heart.

"I fell in love with Ronnie immediately," Nancy recalled.

"He proposed one night at my apartment in Westwood and then called my father in Chicago and asked for his permission. Ronnie had been divorced and he didn't want to make another mistake. I wanted to be sure, too, but in fact I knew right away that I wanted to marry him. I thought he was pretty wonderful and I still do."

Once Ronnie knew his mind, the couple moved quickly. Nancy did not want a big public wedding any more than Ronnie did—at least that was what she later indicated to the world when anyone asked. She did not, certainly, *get* a big wedding.

They were married on March 4, 1952, at the Little Brown Church in the Valley, with the Reverend Mr. Lewis in attendance. Ardis and Bill Holden were matron of honor and best man. It was a very simple wedding.

The ceremony was over very quickly. Nancy seemed to go through it in a sort of daze. When Bill Holden leaned over and said, "Let me be the first to kiss the bride," Nancy panicked and drew back, motioning him to wait—as if the ceremony were not already over.

"You're jumping the gun," she told him.

"I am not!" Holden laughed and kissed her.

So did Ardis—and finally Ronnie.

It was indeed all over. They were married, and quite soon they were driving back to the Holden home near Toluca Lake in the Caddy convertible. At the Holdens' they ate a piece of the wedding cake and sat around awhile laughing and joking, and finally Ronnie and Nancy got into the car and drove off into the night.

They were headed for Phoenix, Arizona, where Nancy's mother and father traditionally spent a spring vacation. The idea was for the newlyweds to meet the Davises during the latter days of their honeymoon.

The Reagans spent their wedding night in the Riverside Inn in Riverside, California. The next morning, after a leisurely breakfast, they drove on to Phoenix, where they checked into the Arizona Biltmore.

"Having a honeymoon with your parents may seem strange

to some people," Nancy wrote later, "but somehow it seemed perfectly natural to us."

Ronnie took the situation completely in stride. His own mother had not been able to attend the wedding because of her health.

Ronnie had never met the Davises, but had formed his own picture of them from Nancy's descriptions. He was particularly impressed by Edie—as he called Dee Dee—considering her personable, friendly, and amiable. He could see how she resembled his own mother in her very unselfish and outgoing manner.

To Edie Davis, the cab driver, the cop on the beat, and the girl in the department store were all on a similar level with her. There simply wasn't a snobbish bone anywhere in her body.

He loved her way with words, too—much like his own. "What a politician was lost in her!" he told Nancy after he had met her.

And Dr. Loyal Davis impressed him favorably, too. He could understand his somewhat austere, patrician ways. He realized that Davis was a humanitarian as well as a superior surgeon and a person skilled at his profession.

The newlyweds spent their free time driving around Arizona looking at the sights and basking in the desert atmosphere before their return to Hollywood. The honeymoon was a short one, since Ronnie had to return to be on hand at the set for the beginning of his next picture.

Actually, the honeymoon wound up in a rather rough drive across the Mojave Desert in a blinding sandstorm. During this desperate crossing—reminding Ronnie of some of the scenes from covered-wagon westerns he had appeared in—the top of the convertible split in the driving wind. Nancy had to kneel in the front seat and reach up to hold together the canvas top that was flapping in the wind and threatening to sail away into the night sky.

And yet it was a nice, somewhat theatrical way to end the most romantic hours of their lives together.

7

The Marriage

On the return of the newlyweds to Hollywood, Ronnie resigned his position as president of the Screen Actors Guild in order to be able to spend most of his nonworking hours at home with Nancy.

The first priority of the Reagans was to find themselves a place to live. As a temporary measure, Ronnie kept his apartment on Camden Drive in Hollywood and more or less moved in with Nancy at her two-story Beverly Glen Boulevard apartment. It seemed to be the easiest way to resolve the residence problem—at least for the time being.

In spite of the fact that they were married, both partners continued with their careers. Nancy had no intention of keeping on in the movies if that obligation interfered in any way with her status as wife or mother. Yet she understood the necessity of bringing in enough money to keep the family going.

It was difficult to settle down quickly. The worries about careers and the worries about the future balanced the more practical worries and troubles caused by their nomadic existence. There were times when they went out to dinner—with Nancy dressing at her apartment, Ronnie dressing at *his* apartment, Ronnie driving over to pick up his wife on Beverly Glen, and then both of them finally arriving at a restaurant together.

They began driving around the Los Angeles area looking for a home. The San Fernando Valley was getting more and more crowded; it had led Ronnie to sell his place in Northridge and buy the ranch out near Lake Malibu. Since they both liked the coastline, they concentrated their search in that area, to the west and north of Los Angeles proper.

Finally they settled on a new section that was just beginning to be developed—Pacific Palisades. Because of the rugged slopes of the canyons and barrancas on the western pitch of the Santa Monica Mountains, building costs were high; certain lot sites caused difficult engineering problems that were never really solved, and sometimes heavy rains and mud slides threatened every structure on the hillside.

Nevertheless, they liked the atmosphere, near the ocean and far from the hustle and bustle of Hollywood and Los Angeles. What made them settle on the place on Amalfi Drive was that it was only thirty minutes by car from the Lake Malibu ranch.

Although Nancy was new to living the life of the rugged outdoors, she seemed to thrive on it because it gave Ronnie such a lift. And because neither of them had made any move to give up motion pictures, they found themselves living busy and almost hectic lives. In spite of the fact that they were situated in a secluded area, settling into a brand-new way of life, their days were busy indeed.

However, the motion-picture industry was beginning to suffer from a definite slump, induced not only by the inability of the studio executives to furnish the public with pictures it liked but by a new and formidable competitive element in the communications industry—television. Although motion pictures and television broadcasting were essentially brothers under the skin, they had always enjoyed what might be termed a Cain and Abel relationship. It was Hollywood that originally began the vendetta against television, terming it a life-or-death fight to the finish.

Hollywood's "geniuses," "moguls," or "kings"—depending on the bias of the speaker—had lost interest in the one factor that had always been paramount in making the industry a profitable and exciting one: the public. They failed to note that the people who ordinarily spent two or three nights a week in the movie houses throughout the civilized world were now sometimes spending all their spare time at home in front of a television set, looking at movies in miniature. They failed to note that what Hollywood charged to see, the public could now have free of charge.

Box-office receipts were shrinking. The motion-picture studios were already beginning to feel the pinch. They had earned huge revenues in the heyday of Hollywood's Golden Age; these incredible revenues were shriveling up with stunning rapidity. In fact, it was obvious to anyone who took a close look at the books and studied the figures coming in from the television broadcasters that the money that was adding fortunes to broadcasting was subtracting fortunes from the film industry.

Another unfortunate problem was that the cost of making motion pictures was rising quickly and astronomically. To compound this problem, the pioneer producers—those who had made pictures when the profits were almost limitless—were dying off, or were being forced into retirement by a new breed of producer.

There was a new scene in Hollywood. Free lances—producers, directors, and motion-picture stars—were beginning to turn out motion pictures themselves, without the financial help of the big studios. The results were not always successes. Without the stability and the rigidity of the studio system, one failure could wipe out an independent producer.

Even big stars were anxious to grab at any role that came along. It was the worst of times for actors and actresses like Ronald Reagan and Nancy Davis. Neither had become a "big" name—the kind of name that could persuade a bankroller to ante up the money to gamble on a new "hot property."

Nancy appeared in what turned out to be a perennial favorite science fiction movie, *Donovan's Brain,* a popular story about a mad millionaire who kept his brain pickled in preservative after his death so that he could continue to wield power and clout even in the afterlife. She played the female lead opposite Lew Ayres. The picture was released in 1954—and to this day still appears on the late-late show on television.

She also made an action film in which she played opposite

Gary Merrill. This was *Rescue at Sea*, later released as *The Frogman* in 1955.

Her last motion picture was made a year later, and she starred opposite her husband in real life, Ronald Reagan. This was called *Hellcats of the Navy.*

That movie was almost an anomaly when it appeared. Even the critics were puzzled about the credibility of a picture devoted to World War II naval action being filmed and released in the 1950s. There was one scene in it that Nancy was almost unable to do.

The action had to do with Ronnie's departure to sea in the submarine under his command. It was a location shot filmed on the dock in San Diego. The idea was that Nancy, Ronnie's fiancée, was saying goodbye to him as he went off to risk his life in combat.

"I started to say goodbye to him, and I, well . . . I started to cry," Nancy said later. Unfortunately, the tears were not in the script.

"They had to stop the cameras three times and reshoot it. I know it sounds silly."

Finally, she managed to say the lines without going to pieces, and it was all over.

"I must say," she wrote later, "the love scenes in this film were the easiest I ever had to do."

Ronnie's pictures were not much better than hers, but he continued to make them—strictly for the money. Most of his free time was spent with Nancy at home after work. He had given up his hours with his colleagues—particularly his union work in the Screen Actors Guild.

In 1950, Ronnie had starred in a motion picture titled *Louisa*, with Ruth Hussey and Spring Byington. It was a Universal picture, part of the free-lance deal Ronnie had arranged during his fight with Jack L. Warner. The picture was produced by Robert Arthur. When Nancy and the Arthurs met, Goldie Arthur and Nancy became fast friends, and the foursome were often seen in public together. They spent more time, however, visiting with one another in the privacy of their own homes.

Another film Ronnie made in the same year was *Storm Warning*, an anti–Ku Klux Klan story in which he played opposite Ginger Rogers and Doris Day. He made a comedy titled *Bedtime for Bonzo*, for Universal, shortly before his marriage to Nancy. The star of the motion picture was a chimpanzee. Of all the pictures Ronnie made, this one was the most apt to be shown in the later years as an example of his work—although it was an offbeat picture at best. In it, strangely enough, Ronnie appears to be completely in control of the comic elements of the role and acquits himself as a real motion-picture professional.

That same year he began to sink his teeth into movies that he found more to his liking, because they were shot out of doors and were action pictures. One of these was a western titled *The Last Outlaw*, in which he starred with Bill Williams, an old-time western actor.

The year of his marriage he made *She's Working Her Way Through College*, in which he played opposite Virginia Mayo. Later on he made *Tropic Zone*, opposite Rhonda Fleming, for Pine-Thomas Productions. And there was *Law and Order*, for Universal.

It was obvious to Ronnie that he was not really getting anywhere in the movie business anymore. His early promise had not really borne fruit. It was time to think over his future. For that reason, the isolation and comfort of the Pacific Palisades house became a retreat from which he could contemplate the world and what the future held for him. There were few people around the house with whom to share confidences, but Ronnie and Nancy seemed to thrive on their isolation, and never looked back on the crowded life in Beverly Hills, Bel Air, or Westwood.

Yet in spite of the problems of keeping a career going, life did manage to go on. Nancy's first child was a girl whose name was Patricia Ann; she was Patty in her early years, and later on Patti.

When Nancy came back from the hospital to the house on Amalfi she was surprised to see that a tree had been planted in the backyard of the house as a gift to her.

"I thought you should have some coming-home present," Ronnie told her with a smile. Nancy tried not to burst into tears at her husband's touching and somewhat sentimental act.

Almost on the theory that if you can't beat them, join them, both Ronnie and Nancy made a half-hour television film in 1953. Called *First Born*, it was a typical romance of the period, made for broadcast on the Ford Television Hour.

It was during those rather thin years, professionally speaking, that Ronnie was talked into playing a nightclub act in Las Vegas. Lew Wasserman had been looking everywhere for properties for Ronald Reagan, but had been unable to come up with anything quite suitable, except for pictures that were less than monumental.

One day he telephoned Ronnie in an elated mood.

"We've got just the thing for you!" he told his star.

"What is it?" Ronnie asked with interest.

"A nightclub act in Vegas!"

"You've got to be kidding!" Ronnie cried.

And Wasserman began talking fast. "The money's very good," he said. And he went on, giving the numbers and the schedules, and Ronnie listened. By the time Ronnie had finished thinking it over and taking another look at his debts and his income-tax obligations, he decided that he was agreeable to a try. Actually, the money for a two-week engagement was equal to the total pay he would get for a typical motion-picture contract.

However, Wasserman's first deal fell apart before it was thoroughly firmed. Immediately he came up with another one, and this one did manage to make it off the ground.

The format of the show was basically very simple. Ronnie was to appear at the beginning of the act as the master of ceremonies to introduce the entertainer or entertainers who were signed on at the club. He was then to play a role in a skit that comprised the last act in order to keep the billing—he was slated as "actor" Ronald Reagan—honest.

He appeared with a male quartet called the Continentals, a group that performed as both singers and comedians. Ronnie knew that the hardest part of all was to get together an opening monologue—the stand-up act so familiar now on nighttime talk shows, but which at that time was confined to nightclub acts.

Although the group he was appearing with offered to write his patter, Ronnie decided to compose his own, basing it on material he had used before at benefits and other charity affairs when he had appeared to help out the Screen Actors Guild. He used the one-liners he had saved from his youth and on through his *Reader's Digest* days in the service.

The skit that formed the climax of the act was called the "Beer Garden" number. In it, Ronnie appeared in a straw hat, carrying a cane. The act became a song-and-dance routine, with Ronnie depending on pantomime and an occasional word in a heavy accent to carry the number.

It went over rather well, and the New Frontier was sold out every night the act appeared. One critic wrote that Ronnie, as master of ceremonies and general fall guy, "personally stole the show with a 'Beer Garden' number."

Show business noticed him, too, and in the end he got offers from the Waldorf in New York, some clubs in Miami and Chicago, and even the London Palladium, which contacted him through a representative in the United States.

He turned them all down. Nancy had stayed with him in Las Vegas during the period, and the two of them had a miserable time when Ronnie wasn't onstage performing. They sat together in their hotel room and read books and magazines they had brought along with them, and only went out occasionally to get some fresh air.

Once they gambled, setting their limit at $5!

They missed Patti, who was home with her nurse.

It was in 1954, just after the adventure of the nightclub act, that the Reagans found new friends in Pacific Palisades. The area was growing by leaps and bounds, and new faces were on view every day nearby. Just down the street, within walking distance, the Robert Taylors took up residence.

Ronnie had met Taylor once, but only in passing, and had never worked with him. Taylor's wife was Ursula Thiess, a German actress who had come to America with a contract at RKO. Ronnie dropped over to say hello to the Taylors one night, taking Nancy with him, and the two couples soon became fast friends.

Nancy and Ursula had children of about the same age, and found that they were also very compatible.

Later Ronnie recalled their friendship with the Taylors, their "down the street" neighbors.

"To us they are friends who run like deer from the glamour spots and dress-up shindigs. Like us, they have a horse ranch and know what to do about the livestock themselves. Bob is a handy man in a duck blind or on a hunt, and Ursula is a happy expert in the kitchen. When we have dinner together there or at our place, wardrobe is blue jeans."

And the friendship took root and flourished through the years.

Ronnie was right about "running like a deer from the glamour spots and dress-up shindigs," as he termed them. And that fact was noted about the Reagans by others—especially by the writers who tried to document the comings and goings of the denizens of the glamour industry.

"Ronald and Nancy Reagan agree with people who marvel at their way of life—if turning your back on nightclubs to sit home and play a quiet game of Scrabble is peculiar, then they's just about the oddest twosome in town!" wrote one scribe for a television magazine. "Not everybody thinks they have strange tastes," the writer continued. "Many recognize the straightforward wisdom of the Reagan design for living."

The truth was obvious: Hollywood was a trap for a happy marriage. There were simply too many long nights, good times, and hungover mornings. There were too many parties, too much rushing from entertainment to entertainment, to allow even a good marriage to remain intact.

Nancy had seen too many marriages of their friends founder on the rocks; Ronnie had been through one marriage that had.

"They have deliberately set up this offbeat almost austere way of life," the article writer went on. "They dress simply, live in a house furnished comfortably but not elegantly. Their happiest days are spent on their ranch, where Hollywood seems like the other side of the world."

And so it was.

"They know their lives have a peacefulness, a serenity that few movie people can achieve. They are convinced this sense of normalcy adds new dimensions to their love."

It was never their love that was in jeopardy; it was their life-style and its dependence on their income. And yet in time, even that problem began to sort itself out.

On February 1, 1953, General Electric had begun to sponsor a television anthology—a half-hour drama each Sunday evening at nine o'clock on CBS-TV. These shows proved to be successful and quickly garnered a good solid share of the viewing audience.

The show had no "host" in the manner of Alistair Cooke, who later became the host for Public Television's *Masterpiece Theater*. Each half-hour segment stood on its own, the stories varying from comedy to tragedy, from realism to fantasy, and from action to introspection. Then in the middle of 1954, the top brass at GE, led by corporation president Ralph J. Cordiner, began to look for a personality to host the show, thus making it a more cohesive unit than a simple weekly anthology of totally unrelated stories. What Cordiner was looking for, actually, was the proper image for the show itself, in the form of a familiar and trusted face.

Music Corporation of America still represented Ronnie, with Lew Wasserman looking around for films for him to star in. Cordiner talked with MCA and other theatrical agencies about the kind of host he wanted.

Taft Schrieber, MCA's executive head of Revue Productions—the arm of the company that was now producing television dramas—learned of Cordiner's search from Wasserman and immediately approached Ronald Reagan to ask him if he would like to consider acting as host for the General Electric show.

Ronnie was on the spot. He had a natural animus against television. It had deprived so many of his fellow union members of their livelihood, and had considerably shrunk his own income from the motion-picture business. In other words, he had a right to hate television, even though he had appeared in a half-hour TV show. In fact, he had stated in public and in print that the medium was not being particularly helpful to the American people.

In addition to that, Ronnie was a union man and an ex-president of the Screen Actors Guild. He had been a Democrat since his youth and had liberal leanings that had not been lost on his colleagues.

Because of these contradictions, the negotiations between Schrieber and Reagan would have made good reading in a textbook on hard-sell diplomacy. Each man would move slightly in one direction, but actually be intending to go on a different course. It was essentially a meeting of masked men fighting with invisible weapons.

Finally they found a common meeting ground. It was the amount of money involved. General Electric would pay Ronnie $125,000 a year to host the show. Even in the agreement there was a slight catch. Schrieber was worried about the catch, from the first moment of negotiations.

The catch was that the company wanted Ronald Reagan to be more than a host who would appear occasionally in a role on the show and direct a segment or two. What the company actually wanted was a personality of some stature who could tour the country for ten weeks of the year, plugging company products to the public at large, and acting as a liaison between company executives and the employees on the lower echelons of the corporation.

Schrieber knew that Ronnie had been quite successful on his two-week Las Vegas stint. He also knew that he had appeared constantly for the motion-picture industry and for the Screen

Actors Guild on the "mashed-potato circuit" to speak for the industry.

What he wasn't sure of was Ronnie's commitment to his home life. MCA had been disappointed when Ronnie turned down other nightclub appearances after the Las Vegas success. No one knew Ronald Reagan's mind at this point.

Ronnie was having trouble paying his income taxes, a result of the government's habit of demanding quarterly payments in advance for a certain number of movies he actually might not make during the year. He needed the GE money and there was no question in his mind that this might be the least difficult way to get it. He agreed to the deal, and after a brief discussion and an understanding on both sides, the papers were drawn up at MCA. Ronald Reagan would host *The GE Theater*—and he was to remain in the job for at least eight years.

From the beginning, Ronnie shone at the role. On the theatrical level, he did extremely well, playing an occasional role and directing an occasional segment. As host and "image" for General Electric, he was superb. His introductions were smooth and professional. His face became as familiar to Sunday-night audiences as the voice of Edgar Bergen and Charlie McCarthy had been two decades earlier. Everybody knew *The GE Theater*—millions tuned in every Sunday night.

Yet it was on the company circuit that Ronald Reagan actually triumphed. He started out simply visiting one GE plant after another, eating lunch with the executives and speaking to individual employees. It was Reagan himself who suggested to the company that he could give speeches as well as press the flesh.

Immediately his superiors picked up on his offer, and he was soon scheduled to visit every one of the company's 250,000 employees and speak to them at luncheons and dinners. For the speeches, he simply made use of his old SAG one-liners, and the jokes he and his brother, Moon, used to tell each other— plus a little bit of political savvy that he knew would be appreciated by people working in the marketplace.

Mr. and Mrs. Ronald Reagan cut their wedding cake, March 4, 1952.

Ronnie and Nancy on their 340-acre ranch in Malibu, California, 1956.

A night on the town at the new Cocoanut Grove Night Club, April 1957.

UPI/Bettman Newsphotos

Governor and Mrs. Ronald Reagan gather before their Christmas tree with son Ron, nine, and daughter Patricia, fifteen, December 1967.

Flying home to California after a campaign trip, August 1976.

Ronnie and Nancy dance on the steps of the Philadelphia Art Museum, September 1980. The Glenn Miller band provided the music.

Ronnie and Nancy on their 688-acre ranch in the mountains near Santa Barbara, California, June 1980.

During the 1980 campaign, Ronnie and Nancy share a chuckle as they try out a rocking chair presented to them at the Neshoba, Mississippi, County Fair.

←

President-elect and Mrs. Reagan arrive by helicopter in Santa Monica after a week on their ranch savoring victory in the 1980 presidential race.

Ronnie kisses his First Lady on July 23, 1981, as Nancy prepares to leave for London to attend the wedding of Lady Diana Spencer and Prince Charles. "I love you. Be careful," the President said. Just for the record, he kissed her four times.

Over the years he spent hours talking with the businessmen who ran General Electric. He would talk, and eat, and speak some more. His speeches were simply booster speeches, perfectly targeted at the audience he began to know better and better as he traveled from place to place.

He knew that these people were exactly like the ones he had grown up with in Illinois. He knew what they worried about, what they liked, what they dreamed about. He gave them pretty much what they wanted to hear, because it was not far from Ronald Reagan's mind either.

In addition to these speeches boosting the American way and the savvy and know-how of General Electric, he became an excellent and consummate salesman for the corporation. One well-heeled executive heard him deliver a typical institutional advertisement for GE's nuclear submarine and remarked to a friend:

"I really don't *need* a submarine, but I've got one now."

Since he had started out in radio and knew how to speak professionally, he used that training to consolidate his ideas in preparation for speaking, and then, when he would speak, he would change the wording and the ideas as he saw fit for the audience he was working.

As he continued to flog the GE way of life to the public, he became interested in exactly what the company was doing. He found that he was not quite so worker-oriented as he had once considered himself. That is, he could see the company's side in certain political arguments—a side he had never given much thought to in his early years.

He could now see more clearly why his brother had always tried to woo him away from his early politics. Perhaps, he thought, Moon might be right after all.

It was a great learning experience—a lucrative, creative, and very lucky one.

The only thing that Ronnie didn't like about the GE experience was that he was away from Nancy for two months when he was speaking and meeting the GE employees. She missed him, too, but put up with it because it allowed them to be to-gether for the other ten months of the year. She was also able to appear with him several times as an actress on the GE shows. One of them, based on a story by the mystery novelist Charlotte Armstrong, was titled *Money and the Minister*.

On May 20, 1958, Nancy became the mother of a boy, Ron-ald Prescott, and the family was now complete. The Reagans had both retired from the motion-picture business and Ronnie was on a completely new tack.

The last Ronald Reagan picture was a rather unsuccessful remake of Ernest Hemingway's classic short story "The Kill-ers." It was not up to the Burt Lancaster version made some years before.

The General Electric Theater lasted until 1962. Among its popular westerns were *Ride the Line,* with Broderick Craw-ford and Neville Brand, and *Saddle Tramp in the West,* with Robert Cummings and a young Michael Landon. Other actors of note starred in the productions—Sir Cedric Hardwicke, Ward Bond, June Havoc, Alan Ladd, Barry Fitzgerald, Jane Wyman, Cornel Wilde, Myrna Loy, Jack Benny, Bette Davis, Ann Baxter, and Barbara Stanwyck, among many others.

During the eight years that Ronnie acted as host and front man for GE, he learned all the tricks of the banquet trade: how to conserve his voice, how to fill his martini glass with water until the last reception of the day, how to manipulate a live au-dience, how to read people as they listened to him and deter-mine what they wanted to hear.

More than that, he paid attention to the responses of all those who listened to him and made mental notes about the jokes that succeeded and those that did not. He also learned how to make statistics lively rather than dull. He developed a number of very good tricks known to the communications trade that some politicians simply never manage to learn.

He could think of things to say to an audience that he knew would please them because he was aware of what they *liked* to hear; and he could say things that did not please an audience in order to involve them *against* an idea or a policy.

His own militant trade unionism—what he had believed in and had fought for all his life—became somewhat altered and diluted in his meetings with employees and executives of the large company for which they all worked. Ronnie became a little more tolerant of big business and of executives in general; he became a little more suspicious of liberal policies that had once nurtured him.

He made a practice of sharing his experiences with Nancy when he was home from the road. He talked about the fact that people were different from what Hollywood thought people were. He himself had forgotten about the people with whom he had grown up in Dixon, Illinois—at least, until he had begun going on the road for GE. Then he realized that his Hollywood days represented life in a tinsel factory. He had found himself once again after some years in the wilderness of indecision.

"I'm home again, Nancy," was the way he put it to his wife.

Home was more than just a symbol for the Reagans at that time. In 1956, just two years after he had started with General Electric, Ronnie and Nancy decided to build their own home in Pacific Palisades near where they were living on Amalfi Drive. This time they decided to build the house around a swimming pool; they would make it their own personal house—something they would create from the beginning.

It was Nancy's house, really. She had never had a real home of her own; she had always lived in apartments or suites in hotels. Under Nancy's supervision, architect Bill Stephensen designed a dream house for Nancy and Ronnie. Like most luxurious Hollywood houses, it was constructed around a large swimming pool. But this swimming pool was quite different from the general run of California pools. It was of a somewhat irregular shape, contoured to the land on which it was dug. It was not to be what came later to be known as a "lap" pool—a dive into it, a lap back and forth, and out for the cocktail hour. And it was electrically heated for comfort.

Like most swank Hollywood houses, this one had a three-car garage to accommodate the Reagans' rolling stock.

Like most swank Hollywood houses, it had an excellent view of the Pacific Ocean and a sundeck to view it from. But this view was much more spectacular than most. It was simply a breathtaking look out onto the Pacific Ocean.

Unlike most swank Hollywood homes, this house had tremendous charm. The living room was of giant size, and yet it had a great deal of warmth and a feeling of coziness about it.

Unlike most swank California houses, this one was all-electric—a bonus of its master's job as image-maker for GE. In the dining room, the whole table was circled by reflector lights— three separate panels, one for white lights, one for pink lights, and one for yellow lights.

It became the electric home of the future, with an enormous switchbox on a wall, and dozens of electric gadgets to work almost anything imaginable.

In the kitchen—a giant room—there were three refrigerators built high up. There were two ovens in the center of the room, and two ranges.

The master bedroom was huge, with a giant bed. It had pink carpets, a pink-and-white bedspread, and pink-and-white drapes. It was very feminine, and to compensate for the femininity of the bedroom, Ronnie's dressing room was black-and-brown—very masculine. Nancy's dressing room was white and seemed to be etched in gold.

The electric motif extended to the outdoor recreation area. There was an electric barbecue, and a rotisserie built into the outside wall, with electric outlets everywhere. There were eight separate circuit boxes.

The exterior of the house was a mixture of stone, wood, and glass. There were hedges to keep out prying eyes, and lots of heavy landscaping to hide the house behind—bougainvilleas, azaleas, rhododendrons, and dozens of other shrubs and bushes. Nancy always liked bright, clean colors, and she doted on pinks and red.

In furnishing the house, she concentrated on the colors and the tones she liked. She preferred cushioned sofas and chairs and liked them to have bright, flowery designs. She liked

Chippendale-style chairs with needlepoint seats and had two made for the house when the children were young.

In the kitchen she used red-and-black lacquered Chinese cupboards that would go well with antiques. She was a lover of all kinds of antiques and filled her home with them.

In the main living room, dominated by a huge stone fireplace and elegant ceiling-to-floor windows that looked out onto the swimming pool and the enclosed patio, she put down two yellow couches and a black cocktail table.

She hung pictures on the walls and laid bright red rugs on the floors—colors to dazzle the eye and to paint a picture of brightness and good cheer.

The decor was at once startling and soothing, formal and informal, loud and subdued. The house in turn was contemporary—but modern as well. There was plenty of stone and glass everywhere. It was an indoors house that celebrated the outdoors.

And that was the place the Reagans built at 1669 San Onofre Drive in Pacific Palisades.

That was the house where the Reagans lived during the week. For the weekends, they had the ranch, and there the two of them remodeled the rickety old frame farmhouse that had come with the land, painted the fences and the jumps, and accumulated furniture and furnishings that went with the rugged outdoors.

And when they weren't working on the house or the outbuildings, they were riding through the trails on the grounds.

Meanwhile, the national political picture was changing in a way that was to affect the lives of Ronnie and Nancy Reagan.

In 1960 John F. Kennedy was elected President of the United States. Ronald Reagan continued to deliver his speeches to his GE associates, criticizing government interference and too much politics in public life—to the growing concern of the GE hierarchy. The hierarchy knew it had to get along with the political party in power in Washington, and seemed worried about their image-maker's gibes at big government.

Although Cordiner was still president of the company, he was ill and did not wield as much power as he had when he had hired Ronald Reagan.

On television, *Bonanza* became one of the most popular shows with the viewing public. Michael Landon, who had once appeared on *The GE Theater* in a western, was one of the four stars of the new show, which began slowly to sink *The GE Theater*.

In addition to appearing too controversial in his slams at government—what with Kennedy in office and a reign of liberalism spreading across the face of the country—Ronald Reagan's brand of politics and sociology bothered some of the GE executives who were younger and more "liberal-minded" than Cordiner.

Using the popularity of *Bonanza* as a lever, the company began to lean on Ronnie. An executive called him one day and warned him to confine his speeches to the selling of General Electric products. The point was obvious: no more political comments. Ronnie blew up.

"There's no way that I could go out now to an audience that is expecting the type of thing I've been doing for the last eight years and suddenly stand up and start selling them electric toasters. You'd suffer, and so would I. I can't do that."

The executive was adamant. If Reagan wanted to speak, then he could speak, but only about GE products.

"That's it!" Reagan retorted. "If it's the speeches, then you only have one choice. Either I don't do the speeches at all for you, or we don't do the program. You get somebody else."

Two days later, General Electric canceled the entire show.

Once again Ronnie and Nancy were at what appeared to be loose ends. In the context of their own romance and love, however, they were on as solid ground as ever. Only the economic grounds on which they stood seemed to be trembling.

It was obvious that something had to happen.

And, of course, it did.

8

The Winds of Change

When she filled out her biographical questionnaire for MGM some years earlier, Nancy had written that her childhood ambition was "to be an actress." However, an even "greater ambition" that had always been in her heart was "to have a successful, happy marriage." She even listed some of her pet hates that showed how her upbringing ran: "superficiality, vulgarity especially in women, untidiness of mind and person, and cigars."

Her dreams of marriage in those days were hopelessly conventional, as evidenced by her remarks above. Yet Nancy really meant what she said in an honest and forthright way. In dealing with the problem of the conflict between her career and her home life she had opted quite willingly and wholeheartedly for motherhood over the theater. This was not an easy choice at the time she made it, yet Nancy never faltered. She believed in what she did, and she did only what she believed in—in spite of its seeming artificiality and inappropriateness at the time.

"When we got married, it never occurred to me to continue my career forever. I didn't want to. Marriage was fulfilling and satisfying enough for me," she said later in assessing her actions.

"It was my choice. That was what I wanted to do. I think there has been a whole misunderstanding about it."

Of course there was. There was confusion and disbelief as well. Opting for motherhood and the neighborhood car pool over a career in the 1960s in California was simply not the thing to do. Nancy was sophisticated enough and honest enough to see that in America the old ways were in deep trouble; that the cherished values of her mother's generation were eroding; that there was a whole new world out there.

In another context, Nancy Reagan once said:

"If you ... don't grow and don't learn, you are pretty dumb. I don't think I'm dumb."

She was *not* dumb—decidedly not. She was in a particularly difficult situation because her natural instincts and her basic ideals were going in one direction in the 1960s, and the trends and popular conceptions of life in America, especially as regards to femininity, were going in a diametrically opposite direction.

Everywhere the winds of change were blowing. Those changes had already taken their toll on Ronnie's career as General Electric's spokesman on the air. The old values he stood for and the old values the show stood for no longer possessed surefire box-office appeal. Nor were the old values of home life that Nancy stood for quite as secure as they had once been.

The Reagans' friendship with the Robert Taylors and the William Holdens and the Glenn Fords and the Edgar Bergens was still holding firm and strong, but Nancy was beginning to form new alliances with people she met and associated with informally in Los Angeles—people who were in no way allied to show business. The group to which she devoted most of her time and energy was called the Colleagues, an exclusive and well-off circle of the socially elite formed originally to raise funds to support a halfway house for troubled women.

Known as one of the area's most prestigious charities, the Colleagues funded its activities by collecting expensive clothing from motion-picture stars who might purchase an expensive gown or suit to wear on only one occasion when they might be seen by the public; the gown or suit was destined for oblivion immediately thereafter, hung up in a closet and forgotten forever. Once a year the Colleagues would put these valuable items up for sale to the general public, and the money collected supplemented the funds of the several charities the group sponsored.

It was in the Colleagues that Nancy expanded her circle of friends outside the motion-picture business to include a variety of members of the Southern California elite—social elite as well as financial elite.

She met and became friends with Betsy Bloomingdale, whose husband, Alfred, had originated and developed the Diners Club, one of the first and most successful of the credit-card empires. Then a multimillionaire, he and his wife were among the new rich who had great clout with the socialites in the area.

She also met and befriended Marion Jorgensen, whose husband, Earle, was a steel magnate, and Mary Jane Wick, whose husband, Charles Z., was a Los Angeles producer and extremely well-to-do businessman.

As for the two Reagan children, they were a handful for their parents, even though their ages separated them by six years. Patti's godparents were Ardis and Bill Holden, still fast friends of the Reagans. Colleen Moore was also one of Patti's godmothers. Patti started out in public school in Pacific Palisades, but quite soon Nancy withdrew her and put her in a private school in Bel Air. She wanted her daughter to have the same advantages that she had enjoyed in Chicago at Girls' Latin School. The private school was Dye School, named for John Thomas Dye, the son of the school's founder, and a casualty of World War II.

From the beginning Patti was under strict supervision at home, where Nancy always watched her closely. At school she found life a bit more relaxed than it was under her mother, but not totally so.

Once Ron was born, the pressure seemed to be off Patti just a bit. Ursula and Robert Taylor were Ron's godparents. One year later, Ronnie was named godfather to the Taylors' baby daughter, Tessa.

When Ron was old enough to go to nursery school, he, too,

was enrolled at Dye School and so was away from the house at least half a day. Nancy was now able to lead a freer life.

In spite of the general affluence of the Pacific Palisades area, the place had the air of a typical suburban community. The mothers took turns driving the children to school in the traditional car pools. They visited one another and talked about the ordinary problems of bringing up children as they sat around the swimming pools that dotted the neighborhood.

For the Reagans, it was costly keeping the children in school and running the expensive household on San Onofre Drive, in addition to maintaining the ranch at Lake Malibu. Money was somewhat hard to come by at the time, what with the changing situation in the motion-picture industry caused by the struggle between television and film for the lion's share of public attention. Still, the Reagans had put away most of the income from Ronnie's *GE Theater* days and were in a fairly enviable situation economically.

Nancy was, however, aware of Ronnie's frustration in his inability to find a decent niche into which he could fit. He had handled his tour for General Electric with finesse and had learned a great deal about people and about business that had nothing essentially to do with movie-making.

But now suddenly with the political winds shifting, he could see the emergence of a new kind of "liberality" that depended on government largess to a point where he felt it had become excessive and dangerous.

Nancy's new friends in the Colleagues had never experienced problems of a financial nature. Neither, for that matter, had Nancy. Ronnie had always done well enough while he was working, and up to this point in their lives, Nancy had never experienced the need to economize, either. But there was the future to think about. Would Ronnie be able to get himself a good, high-paying job like the one he had had with GE?

An answer to that question appeared from outside, rather than from inside. In 1962 Ronnie was approached by a group of California Republicans who wanted him to help out Richard Nixon's campaign for Governor of the state against Edmund

G. (Pat) Brown. They had come to Ronnie because they knew he had supported Dwight D. Eisenhower in 1952 and again in 1956 in spite of being registered as a Democrat and in spite of being known in the motion-picture industry as an old-fashioned "FDR Democrat." They also knew that he had supported Nixon over John F. Kennedy in the 1960 campaign.

Ronnie was annoyed at the fact that they wanted to "use" him. "I don't want to be a professional Democrat campaigning for the Republicans," he told Nancy. "I'm going to reregister and become a Republican."

He did so and then went to work for the Nixon campaign against Brown.

Of course, Ronnie's change of party became immediate knowledge among all his friends. His brother, Moon, had been after him for years to drop his Democratic affiliation and become a Republican. Other friends had been after him, too. Dick Powell, whom he had known since his early days at Warner Brothers, had constantly argued with him about politics. Powell was a conservative Republican, like Ronnie's brother.

When Powell learned that Ronnie had changed parties, he chortled and said, "You finally heard what I've been telling you!"

Ronnie shook his head. "It wasn't just you, Dick," he told him. "I began looking at my friends and I began counting heads and I found out that most of them were Republicans. And so I finally decided that I must be a Republican, too."

But working for Nixon was a part-time task and did not last very long. In fact, Nixon lost the election to Brown and announced that he was leaving politics forever—a premature retirement, at best. Ronnie needed something else to occupy his time.

Moon was now making a great deal of money working in advertising. He had become a vice-president at the McCann Erickson Advertising Agency in Los Angeles. Among the accounts he was handling was that of the United States Borax Company. In the early 1960s, Borax decided to take the plunge and sponsor a television show in order to give its product greater sales appeal.

The big television shows at the time were mostly westerns. The sagebrush saga had reappeared from obscurity after an absence from the big movie screens and had also succeeded in taking over a great deal of prime network time on the small screen. In fact, the demise of *The General Electric Theater* had been attributed to the surging popularity of *Bonanza,* one of the prototype television westerns.

When Borax signaled its desire to get into television, it was thinking of the western genre. And when finally the company, with the advice and counsel of its advertising agency, decided what to broadcast, it opted for an anthology of western action stories that would be called *Death Valley Days,* to exploit the tie-in with its product, Twenty Mule Team Borax.

"The obvious man for the job of hosting the show is my brother, Ron," Moon Reagan told his confreres at McCann Erickson. Moon began a market study on his brother's image to see if he would be appealing as a salesman of borax.

"I'd be a millionaire," he said later, "if I had a hundred dollars for each woman who said one way or another, 'He can sell me anything. . . . I would believe anything he said.' I was amazed."

Although others suspected that Moon had interviewed only Republicans and Goldwater supporters, they finally went along with the survey and approached Ronnie to host the show. After a bit of negotiation, Ronald Reagan had a new job—host for borax on the *Death Valley Days* television show. For that spot he was paid just about as much as he had been paid for doing *The GE Theater*—and he didn't have to chase all over the country talking to employees. For the moment, Ronnie's career problem was shoved on the back burner while he went to work every day.

Nevertheless, Nancy knew that her husband was restless. When the two of them talked it over, they both came to the same conclusion—their days in show business *as* show-business personalities were surely numbered, or at least, they *should* be numbered. But what was there to get into? What did an ex-actor do?

Ranch? That was a diversion, and a pleasant one. It was a recreational gambit, a relaxing hiatus that got Ronnie away from the hustle and the bustle of movie work and the crowds of people. The ranch could never be anything else but a place to go to rest, to relax, and to flail away at physical challenges to hone the mind and the body to razor-sharp edge.

The one thing that had proved interesting and challenging to Ronnie was his appearance on the campaign trail for Nixon against Brown. Somewhere in those early years of the sixties, Nancy and Ronnie between them made an open-ended decision. Ronnie's lifelong interest in politics might hold the key to a new direction for him. If it did not, he could always go back to show business in some form or another. But perhaps it might be better at this stage to go on to something else, to see if it would work out.

Why *not* politics?

The whole political world was changing. So was the face of politics itself. In the 1960s it was now more dynamic, more meaningful, more crucial—largely geared up by the promise of John F. Kennedy's New Frontier philosophy. It struck the Reagans that Kennedy's ideas were right, but Kennedy's *modus operandi* was wrong. The promise of future growth and spirit was there, but the implementation by the government tended to stifle ambition, confidence, and hope.

As Ronnie had been telling the General Electric executives in his last years as their spokesman, government was getting too big, too powerful, too enormous to help the people. Instead of making their lives better, it was burying them.

In 1964 it was again Moon Reagan who helped give his brother a new direction. Neil was in charge of radio and television coverage for Barry Goldwater in the election campaign when Goldwater ran against Lyndon B. Johnson. Moon remembered the answers he had gotten from housewives whom he had interviewed about his brother's "appeal." If Ronnie could sell borax, why couldn't he sell Goldwater?

Largely at Neil Reagan's suggestion, the same Republicans whom Ronnie had helped in 1962 came to him again during the presidential election to seek out his help for the Goldwater and Miller ticket, which was in deep trouble. By now Ronnie and Nancy had already come to a conclusion about the possibility of a political future, and so Ronnie agreed to work for them again. He was made state co-chairman of the Citizens for Goldwater-Miller Committee.

He toured the country and made speeches everywhere for the Republicans. His movements and schedules were so wide-ranging and so complex that they confused him almost as much as they confused Nancy. She held down the home front, managing the children and trying to keep them in line and make the place comfortable for him when he came in exhausted from another day of speechmaking and handshaking.

A close friend remembered how Nancy reacted to this new challenge.

"Sometimes she resented having to share him so much. She always worried about the demands on him, whether it was the kids, the speaking dates, or politics. Everybody wanted a piece of him, the way she looked at it. But she knew that he needed something else to do, and in her own way she kind of enjoyed being a star. Now she could be a star by promoting him. It was a pretty good solution. It was a lot more classy than being the wife of the guy introducing *Death Valley Days.*"

And she *was* becoming a star—admittedly of a different sort from the star she had been in the motion-picture business—in spite of the fact that she was not really running for office herself. Nancy approved of the change. She knew that the future might hold a place for them both if he continued to do well at this type of activity. And she could always help.

The windup of the campaign for Goldwater turned out to be the big opportunity for Ronnie. He reworked his old General Electric booster speech to conform more closely to the Barry Goldwater campaign, and scheduled it for broadcast on television in the last several days of the campaign.

He taped it ahead of airing time, went over it carefully, and finally released it for showing on October 27, 1964. It was titled "A Time for Choosing," reflecting its basic theme. But it was the concluding paragraphs that grabbed the attention of the audience.

"You and I have a rendezvous with destiny," Ronnie told the people who were watching and listening. "We can preserve for our children this, the last best hope of man on earth, or we can sentence them to take the first step into a thousand years of darkness. If we fail, at least let our children and our children's children say of us we justified our brief moment here. We did all that could be done."

Barry Goldwater was buried in a Democratic landslide. However, George Murphy, running for United States Senator from California, beat out Pierre Salinger, former press secretary to President John F. Kennedy and President Lyndon B. Johnson. The defeat of Salinger, a favorite in California, was eventually attributed largely to the considerable help Ronnie gave Murphy in his strong California run.

One national magazine called Ronnie's speech "the one bright spot in a dismal campaign."

Within a month of the election, a group of well-heeled Republicans headed by Holmes T. Tuttle, an automobile dealer Ronnie had known since 1947, formed a committee called the Friends of Ronald Reagan and prepared to launch his candidacy for the governorship of California in the campaign that was to be run in 1966.

This was the moment at which Jack L. Warner, who had always enjoyed an ambivalent love-hate relationship with Ronald Reagan, heard that his former contract player was going to run for Governor of California and quipped:

"No, no! Jimmy Stewart for Governor. Ronald Reagan for his best friend!"

In spite of the excitement and activity of politics, Ronnie and Nancy were still living a very secluded and domesticated life in Pacific Palisades. In a sense, Ronnie understood the value of the schizophrenic life—hustle and bustle on the hustings; peace and quiet on the hearthside. He could cut himself off from the large groups of people who were always after him for something after working hours. He could protect himself and Nancy from the invasion of privacy—usually at their Lake Malibu ranch.

However, it was now obvious that if Ronnie turned total politician and tried for the governorship of the most populous state in the Union, he would lose that treasured privacy forever.

The insulated Nancy, who had never been forced into the rough-and-tumble of public life, except in a remote way during her movie years, was concerned over whether or not she could survive. Thinking it over carefully, she recognized that as an actress her own life had never really been all that private to begin with. Now the children were in school and the family was still a solid unit, even though Ronnie had been a public figure already. After some discussion she decided that she could manage it if Ronnie decided to make a bid for the governorship. And the pact was sealed.

What inspired her more than anything was the fact that she felt Ronnie's views on big government were right. The government *was* interfering more and more in the private lives of its citizens. Even though the interference was in the name of security and protection, there was a trade-off that was unfriendly to freedom.

With the money the Reagans had salted away through Ronnie's years with *GE Theater* and *Death Valley Days*, they were well off and did not need a great deal of outside help to keep them going. However, simultaneously with Ronnie's turn toward a political life, real estate values had escalated so greatly that the taxes on the ranch at Lake Malibu were getting out of sight.

The ranch was a wonderful place to drive off to during the weekend to spend the day in the hills and woods, hiking the trails and riding horseback. Nancy had learned that Ronnie was right—the world *did* look different from the back of a horse. Somehow it seemed a great deal more livable and enjoyable.

There were deer that roamed the place, and the two of them

had even spotted a mountain lion on occasion. But, painful as it was, Ronnie and Nancy decided finally that they would have to sell the ranch. It was a decision that they kept postponing— they wanted the privacy and seclusion of the hideaway so that they would be able to rest together and get away from people. And yet the acreage that had been purchased for thousands of dollars was now worth a cool $2 million—and it was costing a fortune in taxes to maintain.

Finally, after desperate consultations and tearful visits to the ranch where they had spent some of the most memorable and delightful hours of their lives, they opted to sell, and in 1965 the ranch became the property of Twentieth Century–Fox, which would use it for location purposes. After all, it was only a few miles from the Paramount Ranch, which was used for the same purpose and lay just to the north of it.

With their money from the sale of the property prudently invested, Ronnie would be able to mount whatever campaign was needed to make the assault on Sacramento.

"We had to sell our ranch at Lake Malibu when Ronnie became Governor, and that wasn't easy to do for we loved it dearly," Nancy wrote in her autobiography. "All of the children's birthday parties had taken place there, and I can still see myself pushing some young one on the swing we had hung from the tree in the yard.

"It's a family joke that Ronnie married me just to get someone to paint the fences. We put a lot of ourselves into that place. But Ronnie [would have to take] a large cut in income when he left television to become Governor. We simply could not afford the luxury of a ranch."

Another ordeal soon had to be faced. The generally secluded life of Ronnie and Nancy was due to change drastically. For the sake of the political campaign that would have to be waged, their privacy and even-tempered life-style would have to change to a kind of roadshow version of Ronnie's *GE Theater*. And Nancy would have to be at the side of the candidate to present the proper picture of *bona familia* to the public.

Nancy knew her strengths and she knew her weaknesses.

She could memorize lines and she could project character for the cameras and for a stage audience, but she did not know how to project her own persona to casual observers. Besides, it was inherent in her that her opinions were private and not subject to invasion by strangers.

She was friendly with many people, but they were people she knew and who knew her—not just anybody on the street. Besides that, she had always exercised care in selecting her friends and acquaintances. Being a piece of property owned by the public made her feel, in a very limited and arbitrary sense, violated.

She also knew that one of her main weaknesses was her automatic reaction to gag on politics. There was something about selling oneself to others that offended her sensibilities; and yet, of course, she knew that a number of very intelligent and decent people were politicians and statesmen. She knew many of them and counted them among her closest friends.

There was also her deep-seated and abiding hatred of criticism. She could not react properly to sniping and carping. Instead of letting a remark pass, she had a habit of climbing the nearest wall. She could not abide the negative and bitchy commentary so common to the campaign trail.

As for harsh criticism of Ronnie, that was even worse. She could not *stand* things that hurt him. It drove her immediately into anger. In spite of the fact that she understood that such a reaction could only harm Ronnie, she nevertheless was unable to react to any criticism of him except by rage.

There was another problem—a very real problem that plagued her then and that continued to plague her for many months and years afterward. She had a habit of listening to Ronnie with complete attention to what he was saying. To her, this was simply the right way to listen to anyone—be it her husband or a total stranger. Yet it was obvious to anyone who saw her observe her husband that she was in total awe of him—as if she were witnessing some supernatural happening or miracle.

She had been sniped at for what was to become known as

"the gaze" in the past. She knew she would be sniped at for it in the future. And yet she knew that it was too important to her husband's future to make an issue of any of these problems.

What she was good at was minding the home front while Ronnie traveled. She had assumed the chore of being the disciplinarian in regard to the children. Ronnie was always apt to let them off with a kind of benign leniency that could easily spoil them rotten.

On the political trail, she was a hound for details. If a mistake occurred, he tended to wink at it; she tended to punish the offender. And yet she was very good at selecting and working with subordinates. Much better than he was.

But how to make speeches for him when she hated speech-making?

Eventually Nancy worked out a compromise with the group of aides that Ronnie chose to help him make the run for Governor. Nancy Reagan would manage her own "speeches." Actually, each speech would simply be a question-and-answer session with the public. In this way she would not need to "project" herself, to persuade or sway an audience.

The campaign moved quickly into high gear in 1966. Ronnie took to it like a duck to water. He enjoyed the give-and-take. He was good on his feet—better now than when he had run the Screen Actors Guild. He had more understanding of people and more understanding of people out in the business community. He had enhanced his own image through a combination of hosting television shows and acting in movies. The secret of Ronald Reagan, however, was that he really lived the character he portrayed on the screen in his early days.

"The Reagan personality has a soothing effect," Stewart Alsop wrote, "like a warm bath. Listening to him talk is oddly relaxing and mildly entertaining—rather like watching *Death Valley Days*, the television show in which he sometimes plays the Good Guy."

Alsop went on to say that the Good Guy image was no accident, but was firmly molded into place by two California political image-makers named Stuart Spencer and William Roberts, who had been hired at $50,000 a year to promote that personality.

The columnist analyzed the Reagan message as a kind of upgraded version of "the speech"—or "Goldwater revisited," as he termed it. Actually, Alsop's identification of "the speech" was right on target; but it was Ronnie's GE circuit speech, not a speech for Goldwater.

Alsop also saw something that surprised him. "What brings audiences to their feet is not the familiar substance"—Reagan's warning of the threat of "the omnipotent welfare state" to rob the citizen of his freedom—"but [Reagan's] style of delivery."

Alsop mentioned Ronnie's love of one-liners, but only quoted one. Essentially, they were what kept the audiences with him; Ronnie knew the value of humor from his early years in Dixon on radio. He was particularly good at targeting Governor Brown: "Keeping up with Governor Brown's promises," he said in one speech, "is like reading *Playboy* magazine while your wife turns the pages."

Another: "The Governor talks about *his* dams and *his* lakes and *his* reservoirs; you have the feeling that when he leaves office he'll take them with him."

Ronald Reagan even managed to apologize for his own lack of political experience and turn it into a plus:

"I don't know of anybody who was born holding public office. I am not a professional politician. The man who currently has the job has more political experience than anybody. That's why I'm running."

And he loved damning Governor Brown with faint praise:

"Well, he's good to his family.... He's put a lot of relatives on the payroll."

He hit at the high cost of living:

"You ladies know that if you stand in front of the asparagus counter at the supermarket these days, it's cheaper to eat money."

Again: "Do you remember back in the days when you thought that *nothing* could replace the dollar? Today it practically has!"

While Ronnie thrived on the road, Nancy managed to survive with her usual courage and diligent attention to detail. She tried to cooperate with Ronnie's aides and tried to see things the way he did.

About her work for him during the California campaign, Nancy wrote later:

"I think if you're very shy or if you really don't like people, politics is going to be a terribly hard life for you. I am a little shy but I really do like people, and now we'd found a way in which I could help."

And: "I've spoken to all kinds of groups and can't say I was ever heckled or treated rudely, even though I'm sure there were some who weren't absolutely in love with me. I never expected to enjoy campaigning as much as I did. I couldn't possibly have emerged from each trip with more respect for the average person, and I'm glad I was given a chance to speak—and to listen."

The two of them would relax together at the end of a difficult day, enjoying each other's company and resting up for the challenge of the next. It was a tough campaign, but it was a successful one.

Ronnie's victory was in its own way an upset—but an upset that was covertly and in actuality in the making from the moment he had declared his candidacy.

The strength of the Democratic Party in California lay in the San Francisco Bay Area—in heavy union membership, in academics with liberal views, in students, in well-off Californians from the old days, and in ethnics of all kinds settled in San Francisco. This was a strength rooted back in the previous century, when the gold rush had made the area a rich and wonderful place to live.

The new winds of liberalism were nurturing the Democratic Party almost everywhere else in the country as well as in the San Francisco Bay Area. But Ronnie came from Southern California, long the seat of a culture that ran counter to that of the more "civilized," Eastern-oriented life-style of the San Francisco area.

The people who were moving in droves into the Southern California towns and cities were the same kind of people as Ronnie and Nancy. They had solid middle-class values and prejudices, and they stuck to them. The sophistication and social liberalism of the Northern Californians was foreign to their natures. They wanted a place to live and bring up their children while they worked at solid middle-class jobs and "got ahead." It was that simple.

No one recognized that the population had changed that much until George Murphy beat out Pierre Salinger. Ronnie's victory over Pat Brown solidified the trend. While government was growing heavy in one sector of society, opposition to super-government was growing in another. Ronald Reagan was standing at the forefront of the new direction. If it seemed to be a backward step to "forward-looking" people, it was nevertheless a very real and solid step, and it heralded a movement.

There was one ironic overtone to the election that only came into view a year or two after the Reagans moved into Sacramento in 1967. For some time their good friend Robert Taylor had been ill but would not see doctors. He had always been a heavy smoker and had continued to smoke even in the 1960s when he was obviously seriously ill.

Robert Taylor died of lung cancer in 1969. Nancy had spent a weekend with his wife, Ursula, at the hospital seeing him just before flying back to Sacramento. By the time she had landed at the Sacramento Airport, the news came through from Ursula that Bob had died shortly after Nancy had left the hospital.

She hurried back to stay with Ursula and the Taylor children. A few days later, Ronnie gave the eulogy, and found it was one of the hardest things he had ever tried to do in his life. He was overcome by sadness and grief and found it difficult to speak.

Nancy and he were devastated by the Taylor death. For years the Taylors had been their closest friends in Pacific Palisades. Now they were in Sacramento, and he was gone.

Both determined to give up smoking. Nancy had never been

a very heavy smoker, but Ronnie could be termed a habitual smoker—enough to cause concern.

Nancy, true to her steel will and iron nerves, gave up smoking cold turkey, only occasionally falling back to a puff or two. She finally stopped and never started up again.

Ronnie tried to do the same thing, but kept falling back into the habit. Finally someone advised him to try the substitution formula.

Interestingly enough, an early advertising campaign had once advised people seeking to keep their weight down to "reach for a Lucky [Strike cigarette] instead of a sweet." Now, with cigarettes proving to be even more detrimental to the health than candy, a substitute formula was devised advising a smoker, in effect, to reach for a sweet instead of a smoke.

Someone suggested that Ronnie keep a jar of jelly beans near to him at the office so that when he felt the urge to smoke he could reach for a candy to munch instead.

It worked.

The jelly-bean formula was even more successful than anyone had at first realized. Ronnie kept the beans always on the desk, using them the same way he had used humor in the past and in the present. When something came up that bothered him or caused tension to stretch the nerves of his colleagues around the Governor's work table, he would pass around the jelly beans.

Munching on the beans tended to defuse tempers and got people to laughing a little.

It was a great image-maker. The jelly-bean ploy was picked up by the press and by photographers, and the symbol of the Ronald Reagan jelly-bean jar became valuable to a man who had started to make his mark on the political front.

There would be plenty of jelly beans ahead of Ronnie and Nancy in the future.

9

The Sacramento Connection

When Ronnie and Nancy moved from Los Angeles to Sacramento, it was by far the most radical and significant change that had taken place in their life-style to date. So far theirs had been a more or less traditional love story. They had met. They had become acquainted. They had fallen in love. They had married. They had had children. And they had created a permanent home for their family.

Now the familiar pattern—the pattern understood and followed by millions and millions of people all over the world—had been broken forever. Ronnie and Nancy joined the select group of people who were not only celebrities in their own right but were movers and shakers of men and women—politicians, statesmen, world leaders.

Their private life would face a formidable challenge. Others living life in a goldfish bowl frequently allowed their intimate relationships to wither and fade; in many cases not even a modicum of affection remained. Yet Ronnie and Nancy were quite confident that nothing would happen to the strong bond of love that had so far joined them together.

Nancy understood how hard it would be to maintain that relationship in the unfamiliar surroundings of Sacramento and among the new challenges facing Ronnie as Governor. She was wise enough to realize that things would be irrevocably changed the moment they settled in Sacramento. The second phase of their life together—the nesting phase—was over. Most people managed to remain in that phase through the balance of their lives. But it was not to be that way for Ronnie and Nancy.

The first problem Ronnie and Nancy had to solve was that of schooling for their children. It was decided that Patti would go to Orme School in Arizona. Nancy's parents knew the school's reputation, and Patti had been to Arizona enough to feel at home there. As for Ron, who was eight, he would go to a small private elementary school called Brookfield in Sacramento. He could live at home and attend classes as at public school.

The second problem that rose almost immediately was the place where they would live in the capital city. There was a residence supplied to the Governor and his family free of charge. This so-called Governor's Mansion in Sacramento, built in 1879, was located in the middle of town, on Sixteenth and H streets, overlooking a filling station and an all-night cocktail lounge and backing up to the American Legion Hall.

In one writer's words, it was "Victorian-ugly," and that pretty well described it. It reared up like some kind of wedding cake gone amok—four unwieldy stories of bulging, Italianate bay windows, topped by a weird cupola extending two stories above the residential floors. Built of wood and festooned ornately with gingerbread trimming and Mediterranean-type wrought-iron bars, the structure was eighty-eight years old—and it looked it. It had served the families of the state's Governors for the past fifty years.

Nancy first saw it shortly after the election when Mrs. Brown, the outgoing Governor's wife, invited her to tour the house. The first thing Nancy noticed was that there were no grounds around the place at all—no room to move about outside. It was not at all the kind of establishment Nancy was used to at the Pacific Palisades house on San Onofre Drive. To make matters worse, Mrs. Brown told Nancy that the house had been condemned as a fire hazard by the Sacramento fire chief years before.

Through Mrs. Brown, Nancy learned of many other problems inherent in the ancient and seedy structure. Governor Brown had tried to get a new residence built during his tenure of office; in fact, an architect had been chosen and plans had been drawn up. However, the projected domicile was so huge and the cost so high that the legislature had turned it down.

What had happened, of course, was that the Governor's new mansion had become a political football. This fact annoyed Nancy, who thought common sense should prevail over petty politics.

"It seemed so childish," she said. "Governors of both parties would be living in the mansion. What difference did it make which party finally got it done?"

In her visit with Mrs. Brown, Nancy tried to murmur her approval, however muted, as she moved through the structure with its fading wallpaper and ancient carpets. Nevertheless, she had already made up her mind to do something about the living quarters of the Reagans even before she moved to Sacramento.

Typically, she did not tell anyone how she felt—except Ronnie. When they talked about it in the privacy of their Pacific Palisades home she became so depressed by the thought of the place that, as Ronnie looked on with great concern, she suddenly burst into tears.

"I'm sure I made him feel guilty," she admitted later.

But for the time being she did nothing about it.

The Reagans dutifully moved their belongings into the mansion so that the transition from Pacific Palisades to Sacramento would be made with a minimum of fuss.

What troubled Nancy the most about the house was the fact that it was made out of wood and could be a dangerous firetrap if ignited—exactly as the fire chief had warned earlier residents.

Once installed in the mansion, Nancy could see how old the wood was and how filled with dry rot. A fire would make the place go up like tinder. Besides that, it was cold inside the house, and drafty, with a kind of eternal dampness that seemed to have settled into its very walls. There were seven fireplaces to heat the mansion—but fire was prohibited in all seven of them by law! In addition, the house had no fire escapes.

She kept worrying about her son, Ron, and how he would

get out of his second-story bedroom in case of fire. Once she tried to pull away a rusted old screen from the window to show him how to open it up. But neither of them could budge either the screen or the window.

She was at home one afternoon with Ron when the fire alarms went off for a practice drill. She led him by the hand down the stairs outside. Once there, Nancy called the fire marshal aside.

"I can't get any of those screens and windows open upstairs. What should I tell my son to do in case of fire?"

"Well, Mrs. Reagan," said the fire marshal, "tell him to pull one of the drawers out of the bureau dresser."

Nancy nodded, puzzled.

"Tell him to hold it out in front of him, run toward the window, break it, and climb out. He'll be safe on the roof outside."

That made up Nancy's mind for her.

"I began house-hunting." She announced to Ronnie that her honeymoon with the gingerbread and fading wallpaper of the Governor's Mansion was over and done with.

Ronnie's aides were flabbergasted. "You can't move out of the mansion! It's a very bad political move!"

Nancy put her foot down. Even Ronnie couldn't get her to change her mind. Bad political move or not, she was going to get out of the place—and she was going to get *him* out of the place as well. She went around the city looking for a suitable place and finally found one with spacious grounds on 45th Street. It was a two-story Tudor-style house, located on the outskirts of town and far away from the gasoline stations and motels that surrounded the ancient Governor's Mansion.

The Reagans rented the place from the owner, paying the rent out of their own pockets. In April 1967, they moved in. It was a good neighborhood for kids. There was a huge backyard, and Ron could bring in his friends to play. He even built a tree house in one of the trees out back. There was a swimming pool, too, around which guests would sit during barbecues and parties with the Governor and his lady.

Although Ron managed the Sacramento years without any

lasting traumas, Patti did not fare quite so well. School at Orme in Arizona was her first time away from home for an extensive period of time without the direct supervision of her parents.

Her new independence more or less went to her head; it was tempting to become her own person—on her own terms. Like many teenagers in the same situation, she chose food as a dramatic method of expressing her individuality. She ate, and ate, and ate.

"I had never been allowed to eat candy at home, so when I started stuffing myself, I gained a lot of weight."

Finding herself suddenly bloated, and not enjoying it a bit, she reacted by taking diet pills and going on all kinds of crash diets to shed the pounds.

"I abused my body, starved myself, lived on grapefruit, and got very unhealthy."

Her heart rate was high, her potassium level was low, and when she visited a doctor, he warned her that she was ruining her body.

"He scared me into doing something." Patti, like other members of her generation, became interested in nutrition, vitamins, herbs, and certain native healing methods. She began eating in a new way simply to make herself healthy.

"The more I got into it, the more I wanted to know."

She deliberately rid her diet of sugar, salt, and white bread, stopped eating meat, and drastically limited her intake of dairy products. Her resulting diet—of wheat grains, soybean products, fresh fruits, and vegetables—became a mainstay for her. She adopted what some might consider a "health-food kick" as her general way of eating, and adhered to it faithfully.

In effect, she *did* use food to establish her independence from her parents—but in a way that no one might have guessed she would. But of course all this was taking place in Arizona, miles from the Sacramento household.

Two years after the Reagans moved into the rented house in Sacramento, the landlord put the place up for sale. Ronnie and Nancy were pleasantly surprised when a dozen or so of their friends purchased the house for $150,000 and rented it back to them at the same rate they had been paying.

When the transaction was complete, the Governor wrote a letter to the group of people who had bought the house for them, sending a copy to each.

"Dear Landlord," the letter began. "Knowing you receive unjustified complaints and undeserved criticism from miserable and unhappy tenants, and having a peculiar sympathy for anyone subject to that kind of treatment, I thought you might enjoy hearing from a happy tenant for a change.

"My wife and I are very glad you bought out our previous landlord. (He should lose the money on the way to the bank.) Somehow, the place looks bright already, possibly because we've painted a little here and there. (We won't knock out any walls, however, without letting you know.)

"Anyway, the hot water is hot when it should be; the neighbors are quiet. (If they complain, they'll get a freeway right through their piazza.) The fuses don't blow, not even with all the lights on, and it's only ten minutes to my job.

"Just changing landlords has my wife so revved up she's pushing furniture all over the place. (Frankly, it gives me a pain in the back.) But we want you to know we love you, we thank you heartily, and if keeping the place real nice will help show our appreciation, we'll do it. We don't even let the dog in the house, and the kids are severely limited.

"P.S.: I am talking to the people I work for about lowering your taxes."

Ronnie's advisers were right. Nancy's summary rejection of the Governor's Mansion as a residence for the Reagans caused a tremendous furor in the press and was the talk of all the politicians and their wives in town. To calm them down, she made a concerted effort to invite them one by one to the old wooden mansion to point out its deficiencies.

It was decided eventually that a group of people would try to raise enough money by public subscription to build a new official Governor's Mansion—one in traditional California-Spanish style, rather than the outmoded Victorian-ornate that had outlasted its usefulness.

A suitable place in a suburban residential area was finally found overlooking the American River. The yard was shaded by beautiful ancient trees, and there was a nice view of the river. The land had been donated to the state, so there would be no cost to the taxpayers for the land.

The legislature approved the funds to build, and the residence was finished some years later. However, the Governor after Ronnie—Jerry Brown, the son of Pat Brown—was a bachelor and chose not to live in it. So did the Governor succeeding him. The house now sits awaiting the first Governor who wants to use it for his official residence.

Ronnie's elevation to Governor had not been a pleasant surprise to just *everyone*. He had come in from the southern part of the state and taken over the preserve of the north political stronghold—which represented the opposition party, of course. From the beginning, his press conferences bristled with antagonism. The media—print and electronic—seemed to be on the opposite side of every question.

But Ronnie knew how to handle people—even people who opposed him. After a particularly nasty series of exchanges at his first press conference, Ronnie grinned and said:

"I'd always heard a new Governor was given a bit of a honeymoon by the press. Fellows, if this is a honeymoon, I've been sleeping alone!"

They were kinder to Nancy, but she was much thinner-skinned than Ronnie. Much of the early coverage of her was laudatory.

One friendly writer who was acquainted with Nancy's father and mother described her as follows:

"Nancy Reagan looks a little like a Republican version of Jacqueline Kennedy. She has the same spare figure, the same air of immaculate chic. I had the impression that even in a high wind, her short, reddish-brownish-goldish hair would stay in precise order. Many of her smart coats and dresses (size six) are in her favorite colors, pink and red. Her handsome face, her large eyes and full mouth, give away whatever she is feeling, at all times."

Another wrote that she looked like a Gainsborough portrait in a Chanel suit (which happened to be designed by Adolfo). She was described as having "small elegant bones, huge brown eyes, teak-colored curly hair," and a certain "remoteness of manner." Her laugh was "bubbly"—a term the writer had borrowed from Nancy's friend Betsy Bloomingdale.

Nancy spoke of herself for the press: "I wear very simple clothes. I don't like the word 'tailored' because to me it means something hard and masculine."

James Galanos, who designed some of her clothes, corroborated Nancy's statement. "I've never seen Nancy go out and buy something just for fun. She buys carefully and wisely, chooses things that can serve her purpose for a good length of time. She knows simple clothes not only look best on her, they also can be worn over and over again—and have each time a tendency of looking fresh."

She hardly ever wore a hat, and for that reason always took very good care of her hair. "The cut is really the important thing," she told a magazine writer, who agreed that its simplicity was what kept her hair "looking so great and well groomed all the time."

About makeup she was reticent. "I'm a soap-and-water girl," she said. "I wear as little makeup as possible."

In fact, her appearance seemed to be the most important facet of her personality as explored by the national press.

She told one of the magazines that her main regret about being the wife of the Governor of California was that the hectic social schedule gave her little time to dress as casually as she might like to.

"We all enjoy ranch life," she told another reporter, "and I'm determined we'll have a family life." She made it a point to be home in the afternoon when her son, Ron, came in from school. And she was always on hand when her husband appeared for dinner. In the case of the Reagans, the general rule was for the Governor to take off for his private home and escape the chores of the office during the evening hours.

There he would lounge around in a robe, read some official papers, and watch television for a bit. Usually he would try to get to bed fairly early so as to be prepared for the day's workload the next morning.

Asked by one writer how he felt about Nancy, Ronnie smiled and said:

"How do you describe coming into a warm room from out of the cold? Never waking up bored? The only thing wrong is, she's made a coward out of me. Whenever she's out of sight, I'm a worrier about her."

Upon being questioned closely about her relationship with her husband by another reporter, Nancy thought a long time and finally said:

"My life began when I married Ronnie. My life fell into place when I married him. He gave me security and peace of mind, and love. I wasn't looking for anything more. I had it."

These words, carefully thought out and spoken with candor and feeling, generated an almost immediate and explosive negative reaction from a large number of women writers and women readers. In spite of the fact that Nancy knew clearly what was going on in the world outside her home—the women's liberation movement, for example, and the changing mores of the American people—she told the truth as she saw it.

Instantly she raised the hackles of those thousands of women columnists and media representatives who wanted to "dignify" a woman's role as an equal partner with her husband, and prevent her from beng subservient and supportive to him.

Nancy's words affected them in the way a matador's red cape would affect a beleaguered bull. And so it was not surprising that many ambitious journalists decided to present Nancy as a "horrible" example of someone too out of touch with reality to understand the real world, too above it to tolerate reality and integrity, too remote to perceive the truth.

"Nancy Reagan has an interested smile," wrote Joan Didion in *The Saturday Evening Post*, "the smile of a good wife, a good mother, a good hostess, the smile of someone who grew up in comfort and went to Smith College and has a father who is a distinguished neurosurgeon (her father's entry in the 1966–67 *Who's Who* runs nine lines longer than her husband's) and a husband who is the definition of Nice Guy, not to mention Governor of California, the smile of a woman who seems to be playing out some middle-class American woman's daydream, circa 1948. The set for this daydream is perfectly dressed, every detail correct. This is the rented house on 45th Street. . . .

"There are two dogs, named Lady and Fuzzy, and there are two children, named Pattie and Ronnie. Pattie, 15, is described as artistic, and she goes to a boarding school in Arizona. Ronnie, 10, is referred to as a regular boy, and he goes to a private school in Sacramento. He is also referred to as 'the Skipper.' "

And so on.

The writer's use of the word "interested" in describing Nancy's smile was one of the hacks in the hatchet job. In other words, the implication went, Nancy was just *pretending* interest. Also, the subsequent repetition of "good" to describe her as a wife, a mother, and a hostess was a deadly swipe at her belief in "good" manners. And then, in pointing out that she grew up rich and married beneath her (citing her father's write-up in *Who's Who* as nine lines longer than her husband's), she became something of an object of pity—almost scorn.

But the *coup de grâce*, of course, came in the final words of that extended sentence, when the writer pointed out that Nancy was "playing out" some kind of vapid dream about middle-class America—the Great American Dream—but not current; rather, "circa 1948."

The rest was frosting on the poison cake. The repetition of the clichés—two dogs, two children—and even worse than that, the description of Nancy's daughter as "described as artistic"—definitely aimed at the jugular. Of course, the reference to Nancy's son as a "regular boy"—as opposed, obviously, to an *irregular* boy—who went to a private school and was called "the Skipper" finished the assault: not your general impression of the kid down the block.

That was just one example of the kind of press Nancy was subjected to in the first months of her residence in Sacramento.

There were less pointed but still cryptically snide writeups. *Look* said of her: "The first impression is dignity—then the quick smile, the brisk, businesslike walk, the low-pitched voice, warm and friendly. Men like her femininity, women her clothes (Galanos). Nancy Reagan's taste and style, in her first ten months in Sacramento, have won professional admiration even from California liberals who dislike her husband's politics."

But the story also quoted two other points that helped fuel the flames of the eternal fire the women's libbers were hoping eventually to incinerate her with:

"When I met Ronnie," the story quoted her, "that was *it.*"

And: "Advised not to 'hero-worship' her husband in public, she replied firmly: 'But he *is* my hero.'"

"My first taste of political sniping came when people said that my watching my husband when he spoke was an act," Nancy defended herself later. "Well, first of all, I think it's only polite to look at the person who's speaking. Besides, I can't really digest what someone is saying unless I look directly at him or her. I've often wondered what those same people would have said if I'd been looking at my plate or counting the house!"

The flap about Nancy's coolness and distance and the Governor's Mansion fiasco soon subsided, and Nancy began another campaign—this one in earnest. She meant to redecorate Ronnie's office at the state capitol.

"It seemed to me that the offices of the Governor should reflect the dignity of the position and the greatness of our state," she wrote, "and I wanted it to be presented in the best possible light."

She found the capitol building to be in a state of total disrepair, much like the Governor's Mansion. First of all, the carpeting, which had been laid in a patchwork manner, with all different kinds of patterns juxtaposed to make no artistic sense at all, was now full of rips, tears, and holes. Worse than that, some of the holes had been patched up, but usually with irregular pieces of different-colored carpeting.

In the Governor's small office there was one leather couch for people to sit in—and that had a hole right in the middle of it, with bare springs showing through, sharp point and all.

She put in red carpeting, stained the light yellow wood a darker color, brought up some old English prints from the Pacific Palisades house, repaired and recovered the couch, and got the Governor a brand-new desk.

Once she finished his office, she found that the next room was even worse. Starting in again, she moved from that room to another until she had the building looking better than it had in years.

One room, the reception area, had nineteenth-century leather walls, with the leather appearing at least a century older than that. By taking it down and replacing it with burlap, she brough the room at least up into the twentieth century. On the recovered walls she hung up some old prints of the early days in Sacramento, San Francisco, and Los Angeles, and pictures of legislators in the 1800s, and views of the capitol building.

Ronnie and Nancy finally settled into the routine of the Governor's office. Yet the two of them managed to retain that small area of their life devoted to their own privacy. "As opposed to [some] women," Nancy said, "my life has always been public. . . . I've always believed that, especially if you have a public life, you must maintain a private life."

The Reagans balanced the public half of their life with the private half at their Pacific Palisades house, to which they would set off every Friday evening from Sacramento, not to return until Monday morning. On some weekends, they would leave on Thursday evening for three days of rest and recreation. This seemed to be a hard thing for professional politicians to understand. From time immemorial, men and women in high places usually relaxed with their colleagues after hours, talking and drinking and discussing the events of the day in the circle of close associates immediately around them.

Ronnie was made of different stuff. He and Nancy went off together, leaving the rest of the pols sitting by themselves wondering where the Governor had gone—but finally reconciling themselves to the fact that he would always be leaving in those hours to spend his time in energy renewal with his wife.

In spite of their visits to Pacific Palisades and relaxation in familiar surroundings, Ronnie still missed the isolation and privacy of the ranch at Lake Malibu. Although Nancy had never really seemed to be an outdoors person, she had enjoyed the peace and quiet of the ranch, and she too missed not having a place to slip off to in order to shed the tensions of public life.

In the late 1960s, Ronnie decided to shop around for another ranch. He and Nancy put down money on 771 acres of ranchland in Riverside County. There were no structures on the site, but the landscape was rolling and spacious.

The two of them took to wandering about the spread on weekends, having little picnics on the grounds under the trees whenever they could, snapping color pictures of the place, and dreaming about the ranch house they would build there sometime in the future—when Ronnie was no longer Governor.

It was one of those marvelous dreams that fortified the Reagans as they dealt with the daily problems of political life. The Governor frequently bothered his friends and associates by dragging out his transparencies and showing them the scenery of the ranch. Nancy shared his dream about the peace and quiet of the future. For the present, when they really needed a rest away from the crowd, they called on some of their close friends for help.

Betty and Bill Wilson, for example, would invite them down to the Wilson ranch in Santa Barbara for frequent visits. There the Reagans would relax in blue jeans and open-collared shirts and enjoy themselves—Ronnie riding horseback and cutting brush, and Nancy gardening or hiking or simply sitting around and talking to Betty.

It was, in fact, Bill Wilson who finally put Ronnie and

Nancy onto a very good thing near Santa Barbara. The Reagans were at the Wilson place one weekend when Bill suggested that they drive over and take a look at a "view" he particularly liked. The Wilsons and the Reagans drove for some distance before Bill turned off the main road and started up a narrow, rutted, winding track, with switchbacks and turns that were murderously sharp.

It was more a trail than a road.

"We were only on it for seven miles," Nancy recalled, "but it seemed to me like seventy."

Even Betty was getting impatient at her husband's persistence in pushing on. Finally, Bill Wilson turned off the road and drove through an open gate. There was a gravel lane that went through a thick growth of live oak. The live oak ended abruptly and the four of them were looking down across a field toward a small cluster of old farm buildings nestled beneath some shade trees in the middle of a rolling meadow indescribably beautiful.

In the distance the Pacific Ocean glistened in the afternoon sun. In the other direction the land sloped off into the Santa Ynez Valley, which crested at a ridge 2,400 feet up in the Santa Ynez Mountains.

The owner of the ranch—688 acres of land stretching out in all directions—was Ray Cornelius. The Corneliuses had built a home away from the ranch and did not live there any longer. A tiny adobe house—the "main" house—stood in a glade. It was almost a hundred years old, Cornelius said. Around it there were a number of outbuildings.

Nancy knew the moment she looked at Ronnie's face that this was it. That was even before they drove down with the Wilsons to the little adobe house and walked in to take a closer look at it. It was a tiny five-room place, but it was cozy, and homey, and very early-California in style.

The living room had not one but two fireplaces: one of fieldstone, and the other stucco. These were the only sources of heat in the house.

The view was spectacular—looking down from 2,250 feet

above sea level, all the way, it seemed, to the invisible coast of Asia.

Although they did not sign a contract right away for the ranch, they had made up their minds about it on that day. Rancho del Cielo—Spanish for "Ranch in the Sky"—would be theirs in 1974, the last year of Ronnie's second term as Governor.

And it was actually a steal at $526,600.

Fixing up the adobe hacienda and turning it into a home away from home became a do-it-yourself project for the new owners from the moment they took possession. They would drive down from Sacramento every weekend to paint, to tile, and to put up an enclosed patio attached to the house.

Soon, Ronnie bought himself a few head of cattle and some horses for riding. There was an orchard nearby, and an old vegetable garden, which soon became Nancy's main concern. There was a great deal of work to be done around the place, inside and out, and when they had the inside painted and redecorated and furnished, Ronnie began building fences to replace the ones that had rotted away years before. He had to add a workshop for his tools, and then he began clearing some old trails so he could ride horseback through the acreage.

"The Governor rubs the horses down, saddles them, and feeds them," one of his aides who visited the ranch said. "He won't let anyone else do it. He loves manual labor. That's his form of relaxation."

Soon the Reagans dug out and enlarged an old dried-up pond and filled it with water from a nearby creek. They called the pond Lake Lucky and stocked it with goldfish.

The first year building the fence for the corral took most of Ronnie's time. He hired a full-time ranch hand to take care of the place during the days the Reagans weren't there. When Ronnie was in residence, he and the ranch hand cut telephone poles and dug holes to sink them in as corral posts.

The rest of his spare time Ronnie spent cutting the scrub oak and madrone pine to use as firewood in the house to heat it up at night. Even in the summer the Santa Ynez nights were chilly.

"Everybody has to have a place to unwind, and this is ours," Nancy told her friends. Because of the size of the house, it was impossible to have many guests. It was really a place for Ronnie and Nancy to be alone together.

A typical day at Rancho del Cielo would begin about seven-thirty in the morning, with a breakfast of eggs and toast. At ten or so, Ronnie would saddle up the horses, then bang on an old mess-hall triangle to attract Nancy's attention, and when she came out of the adobe house with her big sunhat on, he would help her up on her horse.

They would ride through the trails cleared in the scrub oak and madrone stands for an hour or so. After that, Nancy would go to her desk to write letters, and then perhaps walk out into the garden to work at her flowers, or simply stroll about.

Ronnie was off to the fences to check them out and repair any breaks. In the afternoon Nancy might surprise him with a glass of lemonade or some cookies.

At six-thirty in the evening they would have supper, which was never very extensive, but was always very tasty. After that they might watch the news on the portable television or listen to the radio. They might even watch a movie on TV, and if they did, they would share a bowl of popcorn.

Lights out at ten o'clock was a must, to prepare for the following day. When they left the ranch after two or three days of this, they felt a sense of renewal from head to toe.

"We did it all ourselves," Nancy pointed out to friends, referring to the refurbishing and improvements to the facilities. "We used to come down from Sacramento on the weekends and work all day—then sit by the fire and eat hot dogs at night."

The Governor's associates knew how much the ranch meant to Ronnie. "He *loves* it; [Nancy] just, well, *likes* it."

William French Smith, a friend and associate who became a prominent aide in Washington and later Attorney General, said: "He would be lost without the ranch. He loves the land, he loves horses, he loves digging post holes."

Sometimes Ronnie would get out one of his target pistols and plink away at tin cans set up on rocks in the woods. By the time he had entered his second term as Governor, Secret Service protection had been increased for all public figures—due in large part to concern over the assassinations of Martin Luther King and Robert F. Kennedy in 1968.

"I wanted to try hip shooting," Ronnie recalled, "so I went into a crouch and blazed away and didn't hit the can."

One of the agents who was in attendance with him during his ranch weekends stepped up and stood straight upright beside him, unsheathed his weapon, held it at his hip, seemingly without aiming it, and fired. The can jumped off the rock. And again—another can bit the dust. And a third.

"Well," Ronnie observed. "You didn't crouch."

The operative shrugged. "We lose our rating if we crouch."

Another agent nearby had been listening. "Governor," he explained, "if we're ever shooting at anyone, we're between him and his target."

"I fell in love with those guys after that," Ronnie said. At that time he had no inkling that a Secret Service agent would be following those orders to a T one rainy March day in 1981 in Washington, D. C.

Rancho del Cielo wasn't all post-hole digging, riding, and shooting from the hip. On the Reagans' twenty-fifth wedding anniversary, Ronnie had a surprise for Nancy.

"When I was little," Nancy had once told him, "I thought that when somebody asked you to marry him, he took you out in a canoe and played the ukulele while you dragged your hand in the water."

Ronnie reminded her of that in 1977, and took her out to Lake Lucky, their little pond. Tied to the shore was a canoe— named *Truluv*—and Ronnie grasped her hand and turned her toward him.

"I don't have a ukulele, but I have a harmonica," he said with a grin.

"That'll do," she assured him.

And they paddled out to the middle of the lake in *Truluv*, where Ronnie serenaded her properly some twenty-five years after he had asked her to marry him.

10

Stagecoach East

In 1967 a reporter was badgering Governor Reagan about rumors of his "political ambitions" in regard to Washington.

"The Gallup poll shows that your popularity as a potential presidential candidate is slipping," was the way he put it. "How do you explain that?"

The Governor responded smoothly:

"I regard that as a tribute to my efforts to convince people I'm *not* a candidate."

Even on the night in 1966 when Ronald Reagan was elected Governor of California, an enthusiastic supporter at the victory celebration had unfurled a hand-painted "Reagan for President" banner. At the time it appeared to be no more than wishful thinking by an ardent Reaganite. But seen in retrospect from the late sixties and early seventies, it began to look as if even Ronnie had been casting at least one eye on the presidency for a much longer time than many people realized. That was the reason he chose to be so disarming about it at his news conference.

"The man does not seek the office," he said on several occasions. "The office seeks the man." To a degree, to a degree— that was the unstated but understood qualification of the original adage.

The truth was that the presidency had always been in the back of the minds of Ronnie's main supporters. In fact, most of them considered the governorship of California to be a steppingstone to the White House. Ronald Reagan was never all that sanguine about the U. S. presidency, nor was Nancy. If it came, then so be it; that seemed to be his—and her—attitude.

Yet his handy victory over Pat Brown in 1966 gave his aides hope that he would easily make the transition from regional figure to national figure while he sat in his office in Sacramento. In 1968 the time seemed ripe to some of them for their candidate to make a try for the big office on Pennsylvania Avenue. If it seemed ripe to them, it did not to Ronnie, but nevertheless he allowed himself to be talked into a rather weakly organized try for the presidential nomination.

From the start the endeavor was nothing more than a forlorn hope. The Reagan camp made the fatal error of waiting until the opening of the Republican National Convention to announce for Ronald Reagan—and by then it was too late to stop the nomination of Richard Nixon, who won handily on the first roll-call vote. Ronnie then requested that Nixon's nomination be made unanimous.

The inside story of the abortive attempt at national office showed something in Reagan's nature that was not common knowledge at the time.

"He's an honestly, deeply religious man," one aide said, "and he has a strong streak of fatalism. We kept hoping for a sign—that lightning would strike his golf ball or something—to get him in the frame of mind to make a real run for it. There were no signs, no lightning bolts—and, as far as anyone could see, no regrets that if it were meant for him to be President, he would have made it."

So much for 1968. As for 1972, that was out; Ronald Reagan had no desire to try to unseat an incumbent President. Nixon was reelected in a landslide. Now the Reagan team began looking forward to 1976, when the ending of the Governor's second term in 1974 would give them all plenty of time to prepare for and make the crucial run.

Meanwhile, Reagan was making points in California that were burnishing his name and promising good things for the future. While not actually a great compromiser in the tradition of Henry Clay, Reagan knew how to hammer out deals with legislators. In his administration he turned out to be a much more pragmatic and restrained Governor than his somewhat simplistic campaign rhetoric had indicated he would be.

And he did accomplish important things. He took a hard line toward dissident students and what he called "permissive" educators in the California educational system. He froze state hiring, restraining the burgeoning growth of the state bureaucracy. He turned a treasury in deficit around by increasing taxes. At the same time, however, he started to reduce expenditures in social services, education, and other areas. It was these initiatives, combined with the prospering of the state's economy, that resulted in substantial budget surpluses.

In 1973, during his second term in office, he was able to institute generous programs of income tax rebates and credits and also afford relief in property taxes. The major tax law enacted under his administration introduced progressive features into a revenue-raising system rife with regressive measures.

The most important act of his second term was the institution of the California Welfare Reform Act of 1971, which reduced the welfare rolls while boosting payments to the "truly needy"—recipients of Aid for Families with Dependent Children.

He was laying the groundwork for national candidacy.

"We are being watched," he said in one speech, "watched by those all across this land who once again dare to believe that our concept of responsible people-oriented government can work as the Founding Fathers meant it to work. If we can prove that here, we can start a prairie fire that can sweep across this country."

One political observer wrote: "Reagan's men are dead serious about his national ambitions."

A member of his staff supported that idea. "His out-of-state trips were only taken to places where there were going to be primaries, where he might be on the ballot [later] whether he wanted to be or not."

His second and last term as Governor ended in 1974. The timing was exquisite. His backers had a year to prepare for the

1976 campaign for the Republican nomination. It was decided that the run could be mounted better from outside the Governor's office than from inside it. It would be a personal campaign, with Ronnie building and enhancing his own image by constantly reminding people of his recent accomplishments.

The personal image-making campaign was planned as a three-pronged attack. It involved the print media, the electronics media, and the lecture circuit. Lecture fees would help; without his salary as Governor, Reagan could not otherwise earn enough to take care of his household in Pacific Palisades and his ranch in Santa Barbara.

Michael K. Deaver, one of his associates in Sacramento who had been in charge of the public relations image of him as Governor, and Peter Hannaford, who was working with Deaver, joined forces a few days after Reagan's departure from Sacramento and opened a public relations firm called Deaver & Hannaford in Los Angeles to handle Ronnie's "account."

The triple-pronged image-making mechanism consisted of a once-a-week newspaper column written by Ronald Reagan and syndicated by the Copley News Service; a daily fifteen-minute radio program carried by a 100 radio stations to begin with, but that would grow to 350 in nine months; and a series of public appearances on the "mashed potato" lecture circuit.

The money kept the Reagans comfortable; some of the lectures brought in $5,000 a night! But what was really happening was that Ronnie's image was being carefully molded and shaped to make him appear much more viable for national office.

Once again, the best-laid plans of mice and men, and, in particular, of the Ronald Reagan for President group, did indeed go aglay—with the Watergate scandal turning the applecart upside down and transforming appointee Vice-President Gerald Ford into incumbent President Ford seeking reelection.

Ronnie, whose eleventh commandment was always "Thou shalt not speak ill of a fellow Republican," stuck by his beliefs and made only a muted and ineffectual effort against the obvious candidate.

Yet he did campaign for himself, starting with the New Hampshire primary in February 1976. Ford won that, but by only a handful of votes—a fact that was not lost on Ronnie's supporters. The Reagan campaign made a much more impressive showing in the South, where his conservative speeches and low-profile approach struck a welcome chord. In fact, on the strength of his popularity, the Reagan camp managed to push through a conservative platform at the Republican National Convention that was not totally pleasing to the Ford people.

Nevertheless, for the Reagan team, 1976, even though a defeat, was only considered a temporary setback. On the day after the effort collapsed, there was a $1 million surplus in the campaign kitty. A new group, Citizens for the Republic, was launched in January 1977 to make the push for Reagan in 1980. This group was called "the Goliath of the Republican PACs [Political Action Committees]" by the *Congressional Quarterly*.

It had a mailing list of more than 100,000 people, and raised another $3.5 million to push the total in the campaign kitty to $4.5 million by the end of 1978. Thus the 1980 campaign really began in 1977.

The winds of change that had been blowing in the country in the 1960s were still blowing in the 1970s—but now they were blowing in a decidedly different direction. The sturdy American values that had been denigrated as "square" in the sixties were now becoming stylish again as the seventies advanced. In fact, the struggles of the sixties and seventies were all more or less related to "values" of one kind or another. And many of these values had to do with family and personal relationships and how to deal with other people honestly and fairly.

While still serving as Governor of California, Ronald Reagan wrote a letter to his son Michael, who was about to be married. In it, he tried to express his personal feelings about love, and home, and marriage.

"Mike," he wrote, "you know better than many what an unhappy home is and what it can do to others. Now you have a chance to make it come out the way it should. There is no greater happiness for a man than approaching a door at the end of a day knowing someone on the other side of that door is waiting for the sound of his footsteps.

"Love, Dad.

"P.S. You'll never get in trouble if you say 'I love you' at least once a day."

Because of the shattering experience of his first marriage and its disintegration into divorce, Ronald Reagan knew that the relationship he later achieved with Nancy Davis was one of the most important things in his life—and in her life as well. In that relationship he discovered an eternal verity: that the ability to live a rich and rewarding life was rooted in an understanding of the inestimable worth of *family*.

In fact, in a way much more than Ronnie and Nancy might like to admit, their own family reflected—or perhaps typified—the sometimes unsettling changes that were occurring on the American scene in the sixties and seventies.

Maureen Reagan dropped out of Marymount College in Virginia and eventually moved to Washington, D.C., where she worked as a secretary for a real estate firm. In 1960 she served as a volunteer for Richard M. Nixon in his campaign for the presidency. Later she married a policeman in the capital who was twelve years older than she; the marriage lasted a year. Returning to Los Angeles, she pursued an acting career in dinner theater for a time, then in 1964 married a Marine Corps lieutenant who later became a lawyer. They were divorced three years later.

Maureen worked as a talk-show hostess for a time, and late in the 1970s she became a director of Sell Overseas America, an organization devoted to improving the United States balance of trade by increasing exports.

"My folks were disappointed in me because I wasn't fitting into the recognized world, staying in school four years, and then graduating with honors or something," she said in commenting about her relationship with her parents. Yet Maureen was seen by others as a conservative person with conservative views, much like her father.

Michael Reagan had been adopted when Maureen was a baby and before Ronnie's divorce, which occurred when he was three. He had as rootless a childhood as Maureen. He enrolled at San Fernando Valley State College when he was in his teens, and later went to the University of Southern California, dropping out of each after a time.

In 1966 he was working as a dockhand on the Los Angeles waterfront and became enamored with speedboat racing. With the first $5,000 he earned he purchased an eighteen-footer and began racing.

The magic of the Reagan name inspired a publicist to invite him to race at Lake Havasu in Arizona—at the bottom of the Grand Canyon—and Michael surprised everyone by winning, at the age of twenty-two, the world outboard racing championship.

In 1969 he cracked up while running a 250-mile race in Texas, dislocating both hips and tearing up his back muscles. However, within months he was back in the cockpit again, continuing to race.

In 1970 he married a dental assistant whose father was a professional football player; the marriage lasted one year. Five years later he married Colleen Sterns.

He settled into a sales job, but then launched his own company selling gasohol equipment to farmers.

Michael Reagan once commented: "I didn't see [my father] as much as I would have liked." Yet Ronnie had picked up the children on Sundays and taken them to Sunday school, where Jane Wyman was their teacher. After he married Nancy, Ronnie would take his children to the ranch at Lake Malibu for the weekend.

But in Michael's mind there was always a schizoid quality to family life because he and Maureen really had two sets of parents, not one.

"It was hard," Michael recalled, "growing up in that kind of atmosphere [one father and two mothers], to find direction. Because when you're younger and you live in the big house on Beverly Glen and you have the maid or you have the golden spoon in your mouth and you want a new Schwinn ten-speed and you get it . . . and all of a sudden you reach that age where you just can't live at home anymore.

"And you go out and, of course, you always want the things you grew up with. And you think, 'Gee, I can just click my fingers and it's going to come,' and it doesn't anymore. . . . [My father] would try to explain that you would have to do it on your own. . . . When I was younger, I was trying to find a quick way, and through talking to him I found there really is no quick solution."

Patti Reagan, the number three sibling (but the first child born to Ronnie and Nancy Reagan), attended private high school in Phoenix, Arizona, and then briefly enrolled at Northwestern University. When that didn't work out well, she dropped out and returned to Los Angeles to follow in her parents' footsteps with an acting career.

Changing her name from Reagan to Davis, her mother's legal maiden name, she appeared in several television shows. During the 1970s she met Bernie Leadon, the guitarist of a rock group called the Eagles, fell in love, moved in with him, and began writing songs. One of them, "I Wish You Peace," was recorded by the Eagles.

Of all the Reagan children, Patti strayed the farthest from the mainstream. As an undergraduate at Northwestern, she looked on her father, then Governor of California, as "the enemy."

But once she made up with her parents and moved back home with them in Pacific Palisades in the late 1970s, she changed. There were more long horseback rides with her father, just as there had been on the family ranch at Lake Malibu when she was growing up.

"Everything I know about the land or about nature I learned from him," she said. And he inspired her in dramatics as well.

"He's a very good, instinctive actor. He helped put me in touch with that in me. He taught me you have to believe in your part or no one else will."

The fourth Reagan offspring, Ron Reagan, dropped out of Yale to take up a career in ballet at the Joffrey II in New York in the late seventies.

Ron—"the Skipper"—grew up almost as an only child. Patti was in Arizona at school, and Maureen and Michael were grown up and gone. He was taught to ride horseback by his father.

Like his brother Michael, Ron played football in high school. He entered Yale after high school but stayed there only one semester. He dropped out to study dancing and returned to the West Coast. A great deal was written in the press about his choice of a career, with opposition politicians making as much hay as they could out of it.

He supported himself with odd jobs, like selling men's wear at I. Magnin on Wilshire Boulevard, until he was able to get a scholarship at the Stanley Holden Dance Center. It was there that he met another aspiring dancer named Doria Palmieri. She was a philosophy graduate from California State University at Northridge. One of their first dates was to see a horror film called *Halloween*.

Soon they were dating steadily. It was at about this time that a series of brush fires began raging through the foothills of Los Angeles, including Pacific Palisades, and Ron's mother telephoned.

"We're loading up the station wagon," she told him. "Come over. We need your help."

At the Pacific Palisades house Ron hurried off with others to fight the fire, while Doria was left there alone with Nancy and Ronnie.

"Ron's dad was great," she said. "Really friendly. He sat me down on the patio and told me all kinds of Hollywood stories and then took out these maps so we could study the route of the fire. He was wonderful."

But Ron had never had any differences with his father. Even

when he opted not to campaign actively for his father in 1976, he had explained:

"My relationship with my father is not based on my going out and selling him. And my father and I do have a very good relationship."

In fact, it had been Ronnie who suggested to his son that he discuss the profession of dancing with his friend Gene Kelly— which, in fact, Ron had done.

"I don't care about being famous or anything like that," Ron said. "I just want the personal satisfaction of being respected by other dancers. That's what's good about ballet—no one can say you're only there because of who your father is. You can either do it, or you can't."

With their own values clearly defined and their accomplishments obvious, Ronnie and Nancy must have felt a pang of concern about the paths the four children had taken. Both Ronnie and Nancy finished college and graduated. None of the Reagan children did. It was obvious that Ronnie and Nancy should feel some frustration about the fact that their children had not followed in their well-beaten paths.

"I think if the Reagans could have had it another way, they would have," one close friend said. "But the basic thing is, they love these kids. They're their kids and they accept them."

Nancy wrote: "I think you have to let your children find their own paths and their own lives. . . . I'm sure we've all had some disappointments, large or small, from some of the choices our children have made as they were growing up."

Thus the years between the governorship and the presidency were crucial ones for both Ronnie and Nancy. Specifically, the basic motivational impulse to be nurtured and developed was rooted in Ronnie's psyche. But much of the energy to fuel that impulse was provided by Nancy.

One key question arose at that time among Ronnie's supporters and aides: Could Nancy, as an ex-actress and ex-housewife of the fifties and sixties, help him, or should she stand aside until after the campaign was waged?

From the beginning, one of the men responsible for making

Ronnie Governor of California was able to see clearly the possibilities that Nancy provided.

"Nancy is one tough lady," observed political consultant Stuart Spencer, who had worked on the first gubernatorial campaign in 1966, "but don't doubt for a moment her total devotion to him."

Other associates felt that she would be a definite asset. They also knew her primary function. She and no one else could renew Ronnie when he was fatigued or exhausted. From the time he first ran for Governor, she made it a point to see that he got enough rest. On one occasion he had lost his temper in public when his aides had pushed him too far and tired him out until he was physically spent. Nancy never forgot that ugly moment and guarded him carefully ever after that.

"Nancy gets very upset when things are reported in the paper that are not what her husband has said," the wife of a Reagan aide pointed out. "Then she gets very hard-nosed about it. The governor lets it roll off his back a little bit more, but she's up-front. She usually goes to the source."

In addition to support and devotion, Stu Spencer saw other qualities in her. "She's a damned good politician with good instincts," was the way he put it. "She has a tremendous feel for how something helps or hurts her husband politically."

The question continually came up as to how politically influential she was with her husband, or how strong a role she had played when he was Governor of California.

"She was always part of the team," said William Clark, a former aide Reagan had selected as associate justice of the California Supreme Court. "Not in a cabinet sense, but she played a role in scheduling. She recognized better than anyone else could just how far we could stretch him."

Justin Dart, a longtime friend and Reagan backer, put it this way: "Sure, she's influential. I don't know of a good marriage where a wife is not influential. But is she domineering? No. . . . There's no ring in the Governor's nose; let's put it that way."

Yet Nancy never let her feelings about the real values in life remain hidden for long. She was always ready to speak about the proper mores that added up to a good and decent life—particularly the kind of life-style she had grown up accustomed to.

"In our travels and in the questions and answers we do," she once said, "I sense a feeling of not only wanting to get back to it, but of striving to get back to it. I see it in young people who are around us asking me questions about marriage, relationships, God, religion, how important religion is to me, do I believe in God.

"I tell them it's very important to me; I do believe in God. I think that a lot of young people—even though they might not have realized it at the time—were really searching for something to hold on to and believe in, and it never occurred to them that it was right there for them all the time."

Returning to Stu Spencer, he learned the hard way all about Nancy's political savvy and her ability to bury old enmities if it would help Ronnie's career.

In 1976, when Ronnie had his more serious run for the presidency, Spencer had been hired by the Gerald Ford people to try to win the nomination for Ford. When Nancy discovered this, she considered it disloyalty of the highest order.

Although Ronnie argued that Spencer was simply doing his job and that there was nothing personal about it, Nancy would have none of that. What annoyed her the most was Spencer's imaginative image-making that portrayed Ronnie as a warmonger.

"Governor Reagan couldn't start a war," Spencer's advertisements went. "President Reagan could."

When Ronnie was out of the race, and eventually when Ford lost the election, Spencer learned that he was on Nancy's bad list.

Yet in 1980, when it became obvious that Reagan's aides needed Spencer's help and asked for his services, it was Nancy herself who approached Spencer.

"Stu," she was reported to have said to him, "I want you to know that bygones are bygones. . . . We need you."

And indeed they did need him. They needed Spencer every

bit as much as they needed Nancy herself. The run in 1980 could never have been made without both Ronnie *and* Nancy as a solid team.

She was his balance wheel. In trying to describe the true relationship between these two, one friend of the Reagans said, "They are joined at the hip. When they go to a party, they're together, although they mingle. She's well-bred, conservative, and not extraordinary except for her devotion to her man."

A onetime aide in the campaign pointed out that the very closeness of the companionship between Ronnie and Nancy, essential to their relationship, often led to confusion about what Nancy's *real* role was.

"She is very close to her husband," said John Sears, head of the campaign in 1976 and for a time in 1980. "People from the outside, seeing their closeness, too quickly assume that she must have a hand in the positions he takes. I've never observed that to be a fact. It has been incorrect, at least in my experience, that she takes a strong hand about issues or anything of substance. Even on the very few occasions when she tried to say anything about substance, he did not take that kind of advice from her."

Nancy herself told a reporter what she thought when she read that members of the press considered her a "controlling woman" who did what she pleased with her husband:

"That's just all wrong. He makes the decisions. We can get into a discussion of how to approach an issue, but the final decision is his. Of course, after twenty-eight years of marriage, he influences me, and I influence him, to an extent. But that doesn't mean that you go in there and say, 'Do thus and so.' That just isn't so."

One associate who followed the 1980 campaign said: "Nancy's political instincts and sense of timing are sometimes even sharper than Reagan's."

A reporter traveling with the two of them all over the country during the election wrote:

"It is clear from the relentless strength Nancy showed in the long months of campaigning that she is far from uninvolved in the grittier, more basic stuff of politics. Indeed, the question asked among her campaign entourage was not if, but how much, she influenced her husband's policies."

Helen von Damm, who had served as Ronald Reagan's secretary for some years, said:

"She happens to lack ... personal ambition. She's totally content ... being there to support the President, to be his hostess."

William French Smith said: "She's not interested in doing things for the sake of doing them. She doesn't want to be the head of the national committee on something."

"Nancy's like an electric light bulb," one of Ronald Reagan's political friends put it. "She's either on or off. When she's on, she's incandescent. She can charm the smallest birds from the tallest trees. But she doesn't turn it on casually."

"She just doesn't wrinkle, through force of will or something," one acquaintance said, pointing out that even after a long morning of campaigning, Nancy looked as if her hair had just been professionally done, although it was known that she fixed it herself on the campaign trail.

For a person who had said a few years earlier, "I did say that I wished [Ronnie] would get out of politics, and I meant it," Nancy worked extremely hard, beyond the line of duty, actually, to get her husband elected.

Why?

According to Nancy Reynolds, a vice-president of the Bendix Corporation who had served as an aide to Governor Reagan in California, "She adores him, and he worships her. It's one hundred percent genuine. She has made life wonderful for him. When he comes through that door, Nancy Reagan is waiting for him. She looks like a million bucks. There's a terrific dinner on. She's the best listener you ever saw. Is there any one of us who doesn't want that?"

Meanwhile, with Nancy in the background lending a hand to the support that was essential to her husband, Ronnie was going on throwing out his one-liners from day to day, winning people over to him with his charm and his good humor and his optimism.

President Carter made as good a target for Ronnie's wit as Governor Brown had in California.

"Depression is when you're out of work," he said. "A recession is when your neighbor's out of work. Recovery is when Carter's out of work."

A reporter in Cleveland mentioned to Reagan that President Carter had forecast better economic times. Ronnie grinned and wisecracked:

"I don't know what country he was talking about."

About Carter's qualifications: "An Annapolis graduate [Carter] may be at the helm of the ship of state, but it has no rudder."

In San Diego a heckler was making so much noise in the front row that Reagan was unable to speak. He stopped talking and looked at the heckler and called out:

"Aw, shut up!"

There was a burst of deafening applause from his supporters.

"My mother always told me I should never say that," Reagan confessed, "but I heard so many like him and this is the last day of the campaign and I thought for just once I could say it."

One of his shortest and best one-liners was:

"You know, I think the best possible social program is a job."

In Detroit Reagan said: "I had a dream the other night. I dreamed that Jimmy Carter came to me and asked why I wanted his job. I told him I didn't want *his* job. I want to be President."

He took a pot shot at President Carter's talk about poverty: "The reason he is so obsessed with poverty is that he never had any as a kid."

More so probably than in any other presidential campaign of the past, the Ronald Reagan campaign of 1980 was run and won on the strength of the love and affection between the candidate and his wife. No one in the campaign could have imagined the run for the presidency without Nancy at the candidate's side.

She gave him advice on the small matters he wasn't interested in—the nuts and bolts of logistics, for example. She gave him advice on how to handle the staff, a factor in campaign life that Ronnie shied away from; he didn't like to hurt people and he tended to drift along with subordinates who were not really capable of doing the job that was needed to elect him President.

Nancy was there by his side at all times, most importantly when he was physically worn out. She gave him that one absolute essential that no one else could provide: confidence, ebullience, and a renewal of energy after total exhaustion.

One good example of the way she managed to help without making any decisions herself during the campaign was the episode involving the replacement of John Sears, the candidate's campaign manager. Sears had been responsible for the 1976 campaign, and when it had foundered, some of the Reagan entourage laid its failure to him. But Ronnie did not. He rehired him to get the 1980 campaign off the ground.

Sears brought in two key aides: James Lake to act as press secretary, and Charles Black to act as national political director. At the same time Michael K. Deaver quit his full-time job at Deaver & Hannaford to devote all his time to the Reagan campaign; so did Ed Meese, who was acting as developer of issues for the candidate.

In New Hampshire, the problem came to a head. Sears thought Deaver was bypassing him and talking directly to Reagan, muscling in, as it were, on his territory. Deaver had known Ronnie and worked with him for years; it was a simple reflex action. But Sears was adamant. In a showdown before Ronnie, Sears demanded that either Deaver go or he would. Surprised and nonplussed, Deaver immediately resigned to keep peace in the group at a moment when everyone knew the campaign was approaching a decidedly crucial phase.

Reagan was stunned. He did not want to lose Deaver. But it

seemed the best thing at the moment. However, there was re-action from Ed Meese, the last Californian in the group around Reagan.

Apparently Sears overheard Meese telling a member of the staff that Sears was going to be fired the day after the New Hampshire primary, along with Lake and Black.

Sears took this information to Nancy, with whom Sears maintained a cordial relationship. He told her that the situation was "not tolerable." There was some discussion about what could be done. Sears said he had a solution: to bring into the campaign William Clark, a member of the California Supreme Court.

When Clark refused to quit the bench to join the campaign, the group turned to William Casey, an East Coast lawyer who had been chairman of the Securities and Exchange Commission under Richard Nixon. Casey joined the entourage and met with Reagan.

Later on, Reagan had a meeting with Sears, Lake, and Black in his hotel room. Nancy sat at his side. The dialogue pro-gressed rapidly to a point of crisis when Sears laid it on the line:

"I cannot work here as long as Ed Meese continues to be in the spot he is in," Sears told Reagan. The implication was clear—it was Meese or Sears.

Ronnie blew up.

"He jumped out of his chair and shouted," recalled one of the men in the room.

Nancy acted as conciliator. She heard all the arguments. "Participants on both sides were probably pretty open with Mrs. Reagan," one of those involved reported. "She was trying very hard to ameliorate the tensions."

The outcome of the meeting was not evident immediately. Later on it would all come out in the wash.

At this time in the campaign an important decision was made that eventually led to Ronald Reagan's victory in the election. George Bush was Ronald Reagan's main opponent in the early days in New Hampshire. A debate was arranged between Bush and Reagan by a local newspaper, which intended to support Bush. At the last minute, the newspaper withdrew financial support, because paying the costs of the event would constitute a corporate political contribution. However, it agreed to sponsor and moderate the debate.

Reagan offered to split the costs with Bush, but Bush declined. Reagan then announced that his group would pay for the event. Meanwhile, the other candidates—John Anderson, Howard Baker, Phil Crane, and Bob Dole—were complaining that a two-man debate was unfair and wanted to be included. Reagan agreed to let them participate, sensing that "fair play" was a good issue on which to stand and not wanting Bush to emerge as Reagan's single strong opponent.

Reagan's group told the newspaper that Reagan was willing to open the debate to the other candidates, but neither Bush nor the newspaper would agree. The situation was up in the air when Ronald Reagan approached the site of the debate in a local high school auditorium. When he arrived, Anderson, Baker, Crane, and Dole were waiting with Bush. The audience was restless, and Bush looked annoyed. His attitude had already turned the audience against him.

The positions were deadlocked when Reagan sat down at the microphone opposite Bush and stared out at the unruly crowd. He appeared to be as undecided about what to do as Bush. The crowd continued calling for a round-robin debate.

Before anyone could speak, the newspaper's moderator called for silence, and in the silence Reagan stepped up to the microphone and said that he felt the other candidates should be allowed to participate. At that point the newspaper's moderator called that Reagan was out of order and instructed the sound engineer to pull the plug on Ronald Reagan's microphone.

That was too much. All indecision left Ronnie. He leaned slightly forward, cool and in total control.

"I paid for this microphone, Mr. Green," he said calmly. And with those seven words, Ronald Reagan took possession not only of the audience at the high school in New Hampshire, but of the nomination campaign, and indeed the campaign for the presidency. By his actions he proved what no one else could demonstrate. He took charge of a volatile and dangerous situation—a situation that could have turned into a public relations carnage for both Reagan *and* Bush—and turned it into a personal triumph.

As soon as Ronnie took charge, the other four candidates *did* walk out. The debate between Ronnie and Bush followed, as order was finally restored. The debate was a clear win for Ronnie. Bush was very good, too—but he was bemused and a bit upset by the situation that he had allowed to get out of hand.

It was a triumph for Sears as well as for Reagan—but it was not an auspicious turning point for the campaign manager. The die had already been cast for Sears and his cohorts.

On February 26, Reagan summoned Sears, Lake, and Black to his hotel room for a meeting. Nancy was in the room with Ronnie. Reagan quickly told the three men that they were terminated and handed out a press release that announced their resignation couched in the usual bland press-release prose.

"I think she really tried to help us put together something that would be satisfactory,"said one of the three men. "But I do believe that stormy meeting [earlier] sealed our fate in the Governor's mind and there was nothing she could do about it. People who don't think Ronald Reagan's a strong person mistake him. He's a very strong person, and where he's made up his mind, neither hell nor high water's going to change it."

Nancy's later statement about the episode was indicative of her ability to see situations as they were and not as they might or should be:

"We tried to work it out, and I tried to be helpful, but by the time we got to New Hampshire, it was obvious to all of us that we were kind of applying Band-Aids. It was a situation that just wasn't going to work. Ronnie decided that, before he knew what the results were, he would make a change, so that if he lost it wouldn't seem that this had come about because he had lost—which I thought was very nice of Ronnie."

The Sears episode was a jarring interlude, but the result had its pleasant aftereffects. Deaver eventually rejoined the campaign, and by then the inner conflicts within the Reagan group had been pretty well neutralized so that a unity could be established for smooth and effective working conditions.

The nomination became Ronnie's with only a token struggle. And of course the election itself was Ronnie's after he had buried his opponent in the Reagan-Carter debates and in the nitty-gritty of the campaign itself.

Shortly after Ronnie's great victory, Nancy received a telephone call from her son, Ron, in New York.

"Mom, I'm getting married," he is reported to have said to her.

"When?" Nancy wanted to know immediately.

"Tomorrow. We want it real simple."

And simple it was. Ronald Prescott Reagan and Doria Palmieri, who had joined him in New York when he had won his dance scholarship to the Joffrey in 1979, appeared in the chambers of a judge to be married on November 25, a rainy Monday morning in Manhattan.

The bride wore a bulky crewneck sweater, blue jeans, and cowboy boots. The groom was dressed in jeans, a red sweatshirt, and running shoes. A Secret Service agent acted as one of the couple's witnesses.

A honeymoon was planned for January in the two-day break during the Joffrey tour of Bermuda.

In January 1981, Ronnie and Nancy changed their address from Pacific Palisades to 1600 Pennsylvania Avenue. Their love and affection had brought them a long way from Beverly Glen.

On February 6, Nancy was working in secret trying to plan a surprise birthday party for Ronnie. The guest list was fairly large, and people began showing up from all parts of the country.

"Ordinarily," Nancy recalled, "Ronnie might have been suspicious, but his mind was on an important speech he was to give on TV on the fifth and not on what I was plotting."

But someone in the press dropped an item in a gossip column about the surprise party. It was even mentioned on the *Today* show that a hundred people would be at the White House to celebrate the President's birthday.

By then Nancy feared the surprise was lost. She had told Ronnie that about twenty people would be in for dinner—and he had swallowed it hook, line, and sinker. That night as they were getting ready for dinner, Ronnie frowned and said:

"It certainly sounds like more than twenty people down there."

Nancy thought fast. "Well, you know how all that marble makes the noise reverberate."

He did not guess a thing until the two of them arrived and saw the huge crowd of guests. He turned to Nancy and chuckled:

"You fooled me."

Nancy recalled that they danced until her feet hurt—and everyone had a wonderful time.

Ronnie and Nancy spent their first anniversary as President and First Lady at the ranch in Santa Barbara. Once there, Patti arrived from Los Angeles, and the three Reagans went horseback riding the next day—enjoying themselves as a family, as Nancy put it.

Shortly after they returned to Washington, Ron telephoned to inform them that he was making his debut at the Met in Lincoln Center with the Joffrey II. And so, on March 15, Ronnie and Nancy were present at a gala benefit at Lincoln Center where Ron Reagan performed in *Unfolding*, a ballet choreographed by a New Zealand dancer named Gray Veredon. Ron appeared with Melissa Zamoia.

When his dance was over, Nancy threw her arms in the air and slumped in her chair. Ronnie leaned over and grinned. "Now I can breathe again."

Later, in a private reception room, Nancy gave her son a big bear hug, and they rubbed noses together, Eskimo-fashion.

"I'm so proud of you!" she told him.

"Were you nervous?" the President wanted to know.

"Very," Ron confessed. "I never danced on anything that big before," he said, referring to the stage, measured at one-fifth of an acre.

It was up to Nancy to sum up her feelings. "This is so wonderful! I see too little of my son."

11

A Period of Unreality

In the crucial and dramatic moment just before the operation at George Washington University Hospital began, the President glanced around at the crowded operating room and said:

"I hope you people are all Republicans."

One of the physicians spoke for the group. "Today we're all Republicans, Mr. President."

Between the time the President had arrived at the hospital to be examined in Bay 5A and his entry into Operating Room 2 for surgery, a great deal of detail work had been accomplished to prepare for the operation.

At the start, there was little evidence of any wound in the President's body. However, once his clothes were sliced away, it was obvious to the doctors that the patient's left pleural cavity was filling with blood. That prompted a search that finally revealed a tiny slit under the left arm that must have been the point of entry of a bullet or bullet fragment.

Further search revealed that there was no exit wound; therefore it was evident that the bullet was still lodged inside the body. An incision was made between the ribs, and a tube was inserted to draw out the blood that was forming there so that X rays could be taken. The roentgenograms immediately revealed that a tiny piece of metal had lodged in the lung tissue. The problem immediately arose: Was it a whole bullet, or was it just a fragment? If it was just a fragment, there might be another fragment somewhere else as yet unrevealed to the surgens. That would mean further search was necessary.

The would-be assassin had been captured, along with the weapon. At the request of the physicians, the Secret Service tried to ascertain the caliber of the weapon—but it took a great deal of time to contact the Federal Bureau of Investigation and then to get accurate information. In fact, the first communication was misinformation; the Bureau said that the revolver was a .38. (It wasn't.)

This news threw the OR team into consternation. Logically, that meant that the piece of metal seen in the X ray was only part of what was inside the body. Nevertheless, the team opted to go in and remove that piece before searching for whatever else there might be inside. It proved in the long run to be the proper decision.

The truth was that the bullet was .22 caliber rather than .38 caliber. It was during the progress of the operation on the President that in an adjoining room surgeons removed a slug from the body of Tim McCarthy, determining immediately that it was a .22.

Indeed, the metal in the President's lung was a .22 slug, but a slug in a shape that made it appear strange in the X rays. It was later learned that the bullet was a "Devastator"—a type of dum-dum bullet that explodes on contact—but the slug had not made a direct hit on the President. First it had glanced off the armored right rear panel of the President's limousine; the hollow-nosed projectile had flattened out and assumed the shape of a very thin, jagged-edged dime. This miniature buzz-saw then deflected off the armorplate, went between the car's body and the open rear door, and entered the President's left chest as he stood waving his left arm high. There it struck the seventh rib, glanced off, and entered lung tissue. By then its velocity was spent. But it had made a hole in the lung tissue large enough to put the tip of a finger through.

Once the President was safely in OR 2, the team incised the abdomen, drained it, and studied the color of the fluid. Within a half hour they decided that the abdomen had not been injured and turned to the site where the metal slug was exposed in the X rays.

Now came the tricky part. An incision was made in the left side of the President's chest to explore the cavity inside. A blood clot now appeared to view, formed by blood flowing in from a hole in the lung. This hole was just about the size of a dime. The metal slug seemed to have been heading downward until it hit the top of the seventh rib, and then it bounced upward.

The problem became even trickier at that point. What if the bullet had entered the pulmonary vein and was in the artery? It might prove fatal to remove it. How important *was* it to get the slug out?

The doctors studied the X rays again, trying to line up the actual position of the slug by comparing the shots taken from different angles. It was a little to the left of where the senior surgeon had been probing. But there was an easy way to find out exactly where it was. A soft rubber catheter was poked into the hole in the lung and pushed gently inward. Following the catheter with his finger, the senior surgeon finally felt the jagged metal.

"I've got it," he said to the rest of his team. And within a few moments of complicated and very gingerly probing, he had it out.

But the isolation and extraction of the bullet was only part of the complicated operation. The President's lung tissues had been badly mangled by the penetration of that flat and wicked cutting edge. He had also lost a great deal of blood between the time he had been shot and the time the operation was finished—two and a half quarts, it was estimated.

A blood test was ordered and it was found that there was an insufficiency of oxygen in the President's system. There was nothing to be done about that except to put him on a respirator and hope that the natural healing of the lung tissues would eventually restore their function. He was attached to an electrocardiograph monitor as well, to keep a check on the action of the heart moment by moment to detect any abnormalities.

The crucial moves had all been made by the surgical team

but now came the long waiting to see if nature would be able to take its course and heal the lacerated flesh.

When she arrived at the hospital that evening around dusk, Nancy was admitted to the recovery room where the President was lying attached to the machines. She was profoundly shocked when she saw his face. He looked absolutely drained of all energy—he seemed only a shell of his former self. She began to weep uncontrollably.

Then she grabbed his arm convulsively and held it tight.

"I love you!"

At this moment the President had just begun to recover from the effects of the anesthesia. There were surgical tubes all around him. He seemed to be hooked up to every machine in the recovery room. But he could still breathe only with great difficulty. He raised his head to look around; a nurse warned him to lie flat.

Was he suffocating? Was it all over? His mind was hazy, but then he felt someone gripping his arm tightly. Through half-open eyes he saw that Nancy was with him. He wanted to tell her that he was all right. He remembered once again that the most difficult moments of his life had been when he was trying to figure out how to tell Nancy about something that had gone wrong. But now things must be going *right* at last.

He couldn't speak with the tube in his mouth. He couldn't breathe, either. He realized they had left him a clipboard and a pen so he could communicate.

"I can't breathe," he wrote.

When he had got the words down, he realized it was a foolish thing to write. The real question was: Why couldn't he breathe? What was happening to him?

"He can't breathe," Nancy told the doctor standing with her at the bedside of the President.

"The machine is breathing for him," the physician told her softly.

She shook her head stubbornly. "He says he can't breathe."

They stood there and looked at the patient in the bed. Nancy was despondent. She had sat in the White House residence for hours worrying about him—worrying and praying every so often because she knew it would help. It *seemed* that he was all right. At least he was alive. But he was only a shadow of himself. She pushed down the sobs that rose in her throat. It was no use going to pieces in front of the nurses and doctors.

Gently but firmly, they urged her outside. She stood in the doorway looking back at him. His eyes were now focused alertly on her. He was making a gesture toward the tube in his throat. She could hear clearly what his mind was saying: "I can't breathe."

The breathing problem continued, and the senior surgeon ordered a bronchoscopy. A bronchoscope is an instrument for examining the inside of the bronchial tubes. It also enables the physician to remove any infectious material that might be present in a wound like the President's.

The picture didn't look bad.

But the President still had trouble breathing. By midnight the tranquilizers he had been given had worn off enough to make him alert. He indicated that he wanted the tube taken out of his throat. The nurses shook their heads. He subsided. He stared at the ceiling grimly and reached for the clipboard.

"All in all," he wrote, vaguely remembering an old W. C. Fields routine—something about spending a long weekend yesterday in Philadelphia—"I'd rather be in Philadelphia."

He got a chorus of appreciative chuckles from the nurses and doctors around him.

Now that he was fully conscious, Ronnie knew that he was going to recover. His chest hurt so much that he tried not to think about it at all. The pain came as much from the lacerated lung tissue as from the effect of the rib-spreaders the physicians had used to reach the bullet in his chest. It was best, and it was in his nature, to ignore the pain and concentrate on something else.

He had an audience and he had the floor. He began to put out the one-liners that occurred to him.

His first was the classic reaction to a narrow escape voiced once by Winston Churchill, another master of the one-liner:

"There's no more exhilarating feeling than being shot at without result," he wrote on the clipboard. He did not know— or if he knew he simply ignored—the rather serious "result" of his own situation.

But then he returned to his trouble in breathing and the pain in his chest. He wrote:

"Send me to Los Angeles, where I can see the air I'm breathing."

That got a laugh from the Washington crew, who had read about smog but had never tried to live comfortably—or even survive—in it.

As the retinue of nurses, aides, and doctors hovered around his bed, he scrawled another note:

"If I had this much attention in Hollywood, I'd have stayed there."

Pleasantly surprised at the patient's ability to rise above pain and fatigue, one of the physicians attending him complimented him on being such a good patient. Ronnie reached for his clipboard.

"I have to be. My father-in-law is a doctor."

Then his mind turned to other details that had been bothering him.

"I sure believe in capital punishment," he wrote. "What's this guy's beef? He must have gotten off three or four rounds."

In truth, of course, the "guy" had gotten off six; he had emptied the weapon and had wounded four men—James Brady, the President's press secretary, the most seriously.

"Was anyone else hurt?" he asked.

One nurse told him that there were two others hurt, but that they were okay. She did not elaborate.

"Did they get the guy who did it?"

He was assured that they did.

"How long will I be here?" he wrote.

He was told he would be in the hospital for about ten days.

"I recover quickly," he assured them.

"Good," said one nurse. "Keep up the tradition."

"You mean this is going to happen again?"

It was in the wee small hours of the morning—almost dawn—and Ronnie was going on full steam, in spite of his fatigue, in spite of the debilitating pain in his chest, in spite of his near catastrophe. One nurse laid a gauze pad over his eyes to give him the hint. It was time to rest. Ronnie ignored the gesture. He pulled off the pad and continued with his clipboard.

Finally she shook her head.

"Mr. President," she said firmly, "when I put this gauze pad over your eyes, that means I want you to shut up."

For the first three days after the assassination attempt, Nancy was unable to get a decent night's sleep. All she was able to achieve were short and very light catnaps. She spent most of her time looking out the window, thinking about her husband and his very narrow escape, and about his pain, and about his resiliency, and about his very good-humored way of meeting disaster. He was making headlines all over the world with his—what else could you call it but "heroic"?—reaction to his near assassination. People were quoting his one-liners to one another over the breakfast papers and chuckling—after quite properly gasping at the attempted murder—at the news on television.

She found that she had no appetite at all, and was able only to nibble a piece of fruit now and then. Most of her time was spent at the hospital, where she set up her own command post in a room next to the President's recovery room. She even brought a photograph of the two of them together and set it up in his room.

"I don't want you to forget what I look like," she told him.

The first morning she brought him a pair of slippers, although he was not yet able to get out of bed. And with the slippers came a big glass jar of the familiar Reagan jelly beans, which also went unused for the time being.

Even at that point there were thousands of letters and telegrams coming in to the President, congratulating him on his unbelievable escape from death. In addition to the communications, there were get-well gifts of all kinds—flowers, candy, plants.

She was watching him early in the morning on Tuesday when three White House aides—Baker, Meese, Darman—came in with a briefcase full of papers for the President to sign. In the case was a piece of legislation concerning the price of milk; it was, however, an important bill that had to be taken care of.

Ronnie's reaction to the sight of the three aides was typical of his immediate euphoria:

"I should have known I wasn't going to avoid a staff meeting!"

It was at this time, during the signing of the bill, that Ronnie wrote his name, looked at it, and noticed it was a little shaky. Anyway, he thought, it was official.

For the first time now he was apprised of the fate of press secretary James Brady, who had been shot in the head and had suffered extremely dangerous and lasting brain damage.

"Oh, damn, oh, damn," the President murmured, tears showing in his eyes.

In a later visit, Lyn Nofziger told the President that he knew he would be pleased that the government was running normally without him.

Ronnie quipped right back: "What makes you think I'd be happy about that?"

To the world at large, the President was in miraculously good shape, particularly after his narrow escape from death. In addition to that, the President's one-liners were great copy for the news media to feast on.

The hospital spokesperson said:

"He's on almost no medication, and at this point in time he really probably does not require an intensive level of medical care. He's doing extremely well."

That all sounded fine, but it was a bit more optimistic than the reality of the situation. His prognosis was good—as the statement indicated—but what was supposed to happen and what really did happen were two entirely different things.

Later in the first week—about Thursday—the President began running a high temperature. There seemed to be no reason for it. The physicians gave the President a number of different tests to determine its cause so it could be treated, but none of the tests successfully isolated the reason for the unexpected and disconcerting temperature elevation.

The readings would hover between 102 and 103 degrees. That meant that there might be some kind of serious infection beginning to develop around the wounded area in the chest.

At the White House, the press handout was serene and unruffled: "Over the past several hours, the President has developed a moderate temperature elevation, an occurrence which is considered commonplace at this stage for patients recovering from injuries and surgery of this nature. The President's chest X ray continues to show the left lung to be fully expanded with no evidence of new changes. . . . He feels refreshed and appears well rested after a good night's sleep."

Another bronchoscopy was initiated, but this examination found no infection and yet the high fever continued. The President was beginning to feel the full effect of the operation, and he was aware of the toll it had taken on his system. He was lethargic and very uncomfortable. His chest wound hurt with a dull throbbing pain that he could never really avoid thinking about, in spite of his lifelong training in ignoring pain.

Besides that, he found it difficult to eat. He had never had a really ravenous appetite, but he ate well and enjoyed his meals. Now he simply nibbled at food and sometimes wouldn't touch a thing. He was beginning to stare at the ceiling or the wall most of the time.

Nancy knew that he *had* to eat to recover. And with the mysterious fever continuing to flare up at unexpected intervals, she knew she had to get some food into his body. Instead of the hospital fare, Nancy had the chef at the White House—the

Reagans' longtime California cook, Anne Allman—prepare some soups Ronnie liked: hamburger soup, turkey soup, split-pea soup.

She even alerted West Coast friends who might be flying to Washington to bring containers of soup with them. With this influx of outside food, the staff at George Washington University Hospital began to feel put-upon. But there was no real battle on the food line.

Nancy was worried about Ronnie's *attitude*. He was normally very bouncy and always jumped back from temporary defeats. This time he was not responding, and she knew it. And she was worried. Now she made it her mission to get some food into him. There had to be some way to do it—if only she could think of it.

One evening she greeted him with the news that they were going out to dinner that night. He had been up and around during the day but was not eager for exercise or food.

"Oh, really?" he said to her, more or less challenging her to come up with a good answer or a good story.

"Oh, really," she told him.

"Where?"

"I found a little disco on the way to the hospital."

"Oh, that's great," he responded in a grumbling kind of way that was not really like him.

"Are you going to come along with me?" Nancy was standing over him now, holding out her hand.

"I suppose so," he said, and made an effort to get up.

She helped him, but he shook her off and made it by himself.

"Well, now I've got to get dressed, you know," he told her.

"Not necessary," she said. "Come along."

She led him into her command headquarters. She showed him the two chairs she had set up in front of the big television set. Between the chairs was a table where food had been set out for two. The plates were full of food, but he ignored them.

"What's on the set?" he asked her, as he sat down in the chair.

"It doesn't matter. What's important is the food on your plate."

177

He watched her suspiciously. "What are you trying to do to me? Force-feed me?"

"Come on. I've got your favorite soup here. Now don't disappoint Anne. She made this especially for you."

"Well, sure," said the President. And he began to nibble at the soup.

Although the ploy did not succeed spectacularly, Nancy did manage to get some nourishment into her husband that day. But she was still worried about his constitution. He was simply not as strong as she felt he should be.

Then, quite suddenly and inexplicably, the fever subsided and did not recur. Within a few hours, the patient began to feel a little better. He began to turn his attention more closely on those around him, and even Nancy felt a little reassured. His daily exercises increased and his strength began to flow back.

He even noticed how drawn and pale Nancy was. "He began telling me to go home and get some sleep," she confessed. "He kept saying I didn't need to stay all day."

She knew then that he was on the road to recovery. *She* was the one who needed a good long rest.

By April 11, more than a week and a half after he had been admitted to the hospital, the President was able to return to the White House. In spite of his courageous walk from the limousine through the diplomatic entrance to the White House facing the South Lawn, he was absolutely drained of energy when he finally got to the elevator that would take him to the residence on the second floor.

Only Nancy knew the terrible effort it took him to put on that effective show of good cheer. Only she understood how far down into himself he had been forced to reach to bring out that ebullience and bounce that was his hallmark. He was exactly what she had feared he would be: a shell of his former self. She did not know if he could ever make it back to his former resilience and strength.

In short, Nancy knew how ailing he was still, even though he had survived the assault itself and the aftermath in the operating room. Survived, yes. But recovered? Not quite yet.

He found himself breaking off his train of thought to stare into space, thinking back to some of those crucial moments in the hospital, when he had been lying there not knowing whether he was alive or dead, wondering what had happened and fearing the worst but hoping for the best. There was a certain depression that seemed to hover over him at such times.

"For quite a time afterward," Senator Paul Laxalt of Nevada, a close associate, noted, "there was a certain sadness [in the President]. You could see it in his eyes. It wasn't just the physical pain. I think that he was deeply hurt, emotionally, that this could happen to him, that someone would do this to him. Of course he would never talk about this to us. He is always upbeat, cracking jokes. He likes to recall some of the one-liners he used at the hospital."

In spite of those moments of brooding, Ronnie was able to rise above it as he always had risen above reverses and emotional pain in the past.

It was Nancy, of course, who helped him the most. She seemed to understand when those black clouds descended on him and made him moody and lethargic. She teased him out of it, without letting him know that she knew what he was suffering. It was her love for him reaching out to his love for her—and making contact in those crucial days of recovery.

He emerged eventually from the ordeal with a renewed determination to hang on to the principles of integrity and honesty that had brought him to the White House in the first place. Five months after the assassination attempt, Stu Spencer remarked:

"He's very keen to do what he wants to do. I think he says to himself, 'I'm seventy years old, I almost got killed back in March, and I'm not worried about the next election.' It gives him a lot of freedom."

The President himself put it into words, as usual unable to discuss freely and easily his own emotional and personal thoughts.

"It's a reminder of mortality and the importance of time." Then he smiled. "I guess I thought I was pretty determined already."

It was Nancy who suffered the most emotional exhaustion from the ordeal of the attempted assassination and its aftermath at the hospital. Day by day, even when Ronnie was safe at home in the residence at the White House, her mind would occasionally flash back to the moments of suspense, pain, and anxiety. Then, as she realized she was once again reliving those horrible moments, she would close her mind against them and try to think of something else.

"It takes a long time to realize what happened," she said. "You're in a period of unreality and almost a state of shock."

The toll of the ordeal was not limited to psychological effects. Nancy lost at least ten pounds during the weeks that followed the shooting. It was ten pounds that she was never able to recover—at least within a year's time. Soon she found herself praying for the end of the first term in the White House, hoping that at the end of that time Ronnie would have had enough and would want, as she so desperately did, to return to California and the ranch at Santa Barbara.

The thought entered her mind, not without some resistance, of course, that it would be heavenly if she was not First Lady and Ronnie was not the President. She would admit the hope and briefly toy with it, but then would dutifully dismiss it. After all, it was not up to her to decide. It was up to *him*.

Of course, she had moments of wishing he would not run again, that he would give it up and go back to civilian life. She would think about it at times, as she told Charlotte Curtis in a *Ladies' Home Journal* interview.

"But that was true even before the happening, but, by the same token, he has to do what he feels he has to do. I'd believe that God put him here at this particular time in our country for a particular reason. So a wife accepts that and supports her husband."

During those months she was not able to use the word "assassination" or "shooting." She always referred to the attempt on her husband's life as "the thing that happened to Ronnie," or the date of the attempt, "March thirtieth."

As he struggled to rise above the aftermath, the President could see what a powerful and profound effect it had made on Nancy. Probably, he thought, it was having a longer-lasting effect on her than on him. And he worried about her—especially about the loss of weight she did not seem able to reverse.

"He's always telling me to get some rest and eat more. He tells me that all the time," Nancy confessed during those first days back in the White House.

As for the President, he was able to discuss his narrow escape from death in an objective way—the complete opposite of Nancy.

"I think mine was just a case of [having] to get well physically. When I take off to make a speech and so forth, without her saying anything, I know what a long day it is going to be for her. I just know it by what I can see in her. I wish it weren't that way, but it is."

The effect of the assassination attempt and its aftermath on the public was one of reassurance and relief rather than tension and fear. His recovery was watched carefully and studied in detail.

There had been doubts about Ronnie's age—speculation that at seventy he might well be on his last legs and be fading in the stretch. Obviously a man who survived an almost fatal shooting assault was in much better health than had been originally thought by those who wished him ill.

There had been doubts about Ronnie's personality, too. Was it simply cardboard and plastic—the clever manipulations of a master puppeteer and makeup artist, plus skilled scriptwriters always on hand to come up with memorable remarks? Was there really a Ronald Reagan at all, or was this simply a shell built ingeniously around mist and smoke?

Now there were no doubts. Ronnie's intuitive reaction to

near-death was one of relief and exultation in the form of his habitual one-liners. It pleased people that this man who had been attacked by an armed assailant could survive and joke about his condition while the world stood looking on.

There was also the thought that someone up there must be looking out for the President. Otherwise, why had he been able to survive this attack? Others had died; why had Ronald Reagan lived?

Ronnie's stock rose powerfully during those first months of his administration. Because his stock rose, the honeymoon with Congress lasted much longer than usual. He was able to put over some of his most controversial budget requests with much less opposition than would have been possible had there been no crisis to be weathered successfully.

During the most ticklish phases of Ronnie's recuperation— when he was definitely on the mend but was not able to go on any long trips and was actually resting at Camp David—his daughter Maureen was married in Beverly Hills in the Petit Trianon Room of the Beverly Wilshire Hotel to Dennis Revell, whom she had met eight years before while the two were working as California Young Republicans.

Although Ronnie and Nancy were not present, there were Secret Service agents around to point up the fact that the bride was the daughter of the President. Acting as surrogate for Ronnie was Maureen's uncle, Neil Reagan, who gave the bride away.

The height of the ceremony was a telephone call from Washington, with the President sending best wishes to the bride. Maureen's brother Michael was present, but Patti and Ron, her half brother and half sister, were not.

Accompanied by six security agents, the bride and groom flew to England and Germany for their honeymoon, with the President's best wishes echoing in their ears.

Mother Theresa, of Calcutta, India, winner of the Nobel

Peace Prize in 1979, visited the White House in June 1981, two months after the shooting.

The usual fanfare and hoopla were missing in their very private meeting—attended only by Ronnie, Nancy, Mother Theresa, and one or two others. The President was still lacking his usual bounce and animation, but he was on the road to recovery, and he did everything in his power to make her visit meaningful.

It was toward the end of the meal that the Indian woman gazed at the President and the First Lady and said:

"You have suffered the passion of the cross and have received grace." She looked straight into Ronnie's blue eyes. "There is a purpose in this," she went on, as the President blinked momentarily and Nancy's eyes clouded with tears. "Because of your suffering and pain you will now understand the suffering and pain of the world."

There was a stunned moment of silence.

"This has happened to you at this time," she went on slowly, "because your country and the world need you."

Nancy burst into tears.

Ronnie sank into profound silence for one of the very few times in his life.

12

Encore!

Once Ronnie was definitely on the mend, Nancy began to gain back some of her normal energy and strength. It was almost as if her reign as First Lady had been halted for a lengthy interim even before it had properly started. Although the President and the First Lady went through all the prescribed motions in the months that followed during that first year in Washington, the nightmare of the assassination attempt continued to dog every moment of their lives.

"The first year was terrible," Nancy said. "That year is almost wiped out for me. There were all of those personal things that happened."

She was referring primarily, of course, to the assassination attempt.

"That little episode that happened to me on March thirtieth," Ronnie said with his usual lighthearted approach, "she didn't get over it as quickly as I did."

And there was more to come. One of these "personal things" concerned her efforts to redecorate the private rooms at the White House residence by using $800,000 raised by friends rather than public funds. However, to the press it smacked of conflict of interest. There began a new series of attacks on her for spending so much money—even if it *wasn't* the public's money—when so many Americans were out of work.

"I can't understand why there's so much fuss over the fact that I tried to use money that wasn't public," she told Ronnie.

"Those attacks are uncalled-for," he assured her, "but that doesn't make them any less painful. I know it's easy to say, but

I don't think you should let yourself be upset by these things!"

She sighed. "Oh, I wish I knew how to develop a thick skin," she confessed. "I guess either you're born with it or you're not. I'm not as surprised as I used to be by the cruelty, but it still hurts. Of course, there are legitimate differences of opinion about everything—there should be with the two-party system."

"Not necessarily so about *everything*—especially when it involves an action right out of your very nature. You believe that Jackie Kennedy was right when Jackie once answered her husband about what she was doing to upgrade the White House. She said, 'This house belongs to all of America. It should be the prettiest house in America.' I know that you too feel very strongly about that. You'd be wrong if you didn't!"

"What upsets me is when people get very personal, very vicious, and very sarcastic. I have to question the strength of people's positions when they resort to that sort of thing."

"I wish you could just forget it, but of course you can't. Just recognize that there's going to be some false image-building by the opposition."

Although he managed to alleviate some of her gloom over that particular attack, it was only a short time before another problem arose. This one concerned her purchase of $209,000 worth of expensive china—this money again donated by friends "for the cause."

Again, her hurt brought sympathy from Ronnie, but didn't mitigate the attacks any.

There was more. When someone suggested the President should invite opera star Frederica von Stade to perform at a state dinner, Nancy called one of her aides to her side and suggested that she consult Frank Sinatra about the possibility. Sinatra was a constant visitor to the White House and a personal friend of the First Lady's. However, when the story got out, it seemed as if Nancy were callously fobbing off the invitation of the renowned singer with a casual "check it out with Frank" gesture.

Later, one writer summed up the point of the story in this fashion:

"There is a little element here of Louis XIV's French court and *les précieuses*—the affected ladies."

The writer went on to point out that Nancy, like some of the early French royalty, seemed to like to have witty, amusing, and well-dressed men around who were willing "to walk three paces to the rear."

The media tended to make a great deal of fuss over another of Nancy's personal friends—this one Jerry Zipkin, a New Yorker who was a bachelor, was very rich, and loved to go to parties. Nancy thought of him as a "modern-day Oscar Wilde"—minus, of course, the poetic genius.

The point seemed to be that Nancy did have innate taste, and good instincts—but with great blind spots showing up here and there, particularly in regard to glamour, class, and notoriety, which all seemed to be inextricably blended together in her mind.

And there were still mutters about the amount of money she spent on her inaugural gown. Ronnie simply threw up his hands whenever he got to discussing that special matter with Nancy.

"Listen, if any of those people who are writing about your extravagance in dress knew what they were talking about they would have to laugh the same way I do when I think about it. *I* know you never throw anything away once you've bought it."

Nancy giggled. "You're always telling me I've still got my middie blouses from gym class. Today no one even knows what a middie blouse *is*."

"Well, *haven't* you got your old middie blouses?" the President teased her.

She ignored him. "What shall I do about these press attacks?"

"Forget them!" admonished Ronnie. "You're a warm and caring person and you're easily hurt. You want the public image to be that of a loving and decent person. It seems to come out the other way. You take everything to heart. Too much."

"Oh, dear," said Nancy. "I hate to bother you with these trivial things—but to me they *are* important."

"You can't argue with something that's written about you in the paper or in a magazine. But maybe you can react to it."

"How do you mean? Write an article in rebuttal?"

"No. You once told me that you took a long hot bath after someone had written an article critical of me and simply 'told off' the writer while you were soaking in the tub. Can't you do that for yourself?"

"I'll think about it."

It was, indeed, a good way to get her animosities out of her system. Surprisingly enough, although Nancy had made a habit of holding "marvelous imaginary conversations" with people who wrote bad things about Ronnie, she had never thought of using the therapy in her own case.

She found that she was very good at it—she said everything the way it should be said. "All the words come as they should if you had the opportunity of saying them," she recounted later, "and the other person can't answer back. You get out of the tub after a while feeling marvelous!"

In the fall of 1981, Maureen Reagan—now Maureen Revell—decided to run for the Republican Senate nomination in California.

This posed a problem for Ronnie and Nancy. To exert pressure on the party from the White House would tend to alienate those candidates running against Maureen—and also might anger voters as well who would think themselves being manipulated. Not to push for Maureen would make the President and First Lady look like uncaring parents.

Long and thoughtful discussions went on between Ronnie and Nancy before they decided what would be the best policy in the long run. What actually they decided is not known, but in fact neither of them made any formal or informal statement at all about the primary.

Maureen finished fifth, pulling about 5 percent of the vote.

The decision not to become involved—if indeed that was their decision—must have been a difficult one to make. Their silence did in fact prove unpopular with many members of the press, but it certainly showed a typical Reaganesque attitude toward integrity and independence.

Eventually, with the very bad days of 1981 in Washington finally behind her, Nancy began to shake off the gloom and despair and emerged from her emotional bomb shelter.

"I tended to retreat and hold back," was the way she described her withdrawal.

One sign that her retreat into the inner essence of her persona was over occurred in the spring of 1982 during a night out on the town.

It was Ronnie who in a sense gave Nancy the courage and the inspiration for a "brave new image." During their talks together when he had been trying to show her how to ward off the painful feelings of inadequacy and resentment that accompanied criticisms of her actions, he had once mentioned his own belief in the use of humor as a weapon against pain. Nancy had seen how effective Ronnie's use of humor had been in his recovery from the assassination attempt. She had also seen how appealing his use of the humorous approach was with the public at large.

"You're an actress, and a very good one," Ronnie reminded her. "You've got the talent to make yourself into the proper image. And you've got the talent to cover up any hurt you might feel. Maybe it's hard for you to laugh at yourself. Maybe that's why people pick on you."

It was true, she reasoned. She was thin-skinned, but she was an actress. How could she use that talent to bring herself out more, to make herself more popular?

And so at the Gridiron Dinner, held in March 1982, Nancy showed herself in a brand-new light—in an image that had been suggested in part by her husband.

One of the highlights of the Gridiron Dinner was a lampoon on the First Lady. A skit was presented in which a singer teased Nancy's taste for designer gowns and state-of-the-art high fashion, satirizing her in words written to the tune of

Fanny Brice's hit song of the 1920s, "Secondhand Rose from Second Avenue"—the point, being, of course, that Nancy's clothes were far from secondhand.

The skit was well received and the applause was still echoing when suddenly there was action on the stage with the appearance of a rack of clothes resembling those pushed about on the streets of New York's garment district. Then, from the folds of the apparel on the rack, a clownishly dressed woman emerged in a raggedy patchwork costume made out of typical poor-folks gingham and wearing bright yellow hillbilly boots.

The bag lady began capering about and sang new words to the tune that had been parodied so neatly already.

But this was somewhat different. The actress appearing in the garb of a tasteless bag lady was the First Lady herself—laughing at herself in a most unusual and somehow appealing way.

The words, written by members of her staff, were as witty as the original parody lyrics. As she capered about the stage, she sang:

> "Secondhand clothes, I'm wearing secondhand clothes,
> They're all the things in the spring fashion shows.
> Even my new trench coat with the fur collar
> Ronnie bought for ten cents on the dollar. . . ."

Later, one of the verses went:

> "Even though they tell her that she's no longer queen
> Did Ronnie have to buy her a new sewing machine?"

Nancy's performance—a satire within a satire—brought down the house. The ability to laugh at herself was a new facet in the character of the First Lady. Many in Washington had never glimpsed that talent before. They were properly impressed.

Even the staid *New York Times* applauded her in these

words: "No other First Lady had ever come so well prepared with shtick, even including a mock piece of White House china to smash onstage. Socko!"

After her evening as the bag lady at the Gridiron Dinner, Nancy's personal stock rose everywhere, but most particularly in the nation's capital.

The First Lady had a sense of humor! It was headline news.

But there was trouble of a personal nature to follow. In early August the telephone rang one afternoon. It was her mother.

"Your father is very sick," she told Nancy in a hushed voice. "He's going to have to go to the hospital."

"His heart?" Nancy asked, dreading the truth.

"Yes," said her mother.

Nancy knew that he had been suffering from a heart problem for some time now.

"Keep me posted," she told her mother.

Within days she knew the situation was serious, and was getting worse. On August 18, after several conversations with her mother, she talked to Ronnie about her father's illness. He was solicitous and as concerned as she was.

"You go to Scottsdale," he advised her. "You'll want to be there. If you need anything, call me."

Nancy flew to Arizona to be with her parents, but there was little time left. On August 19, Dr. Loyal Davis died at the age of eighty-six.

Immediately Ronnie was on the telephone to her, advising her of his intention to be at her side during the funeral services. On the next day he flew to Phoenix from Washington. He was there to console her through the bitter hours that followed her father's death. They held hands during the ceremony, Ronnie's grip giving her strength to weather the ordeal. For once the press kept its distance and did not intrude on her grief.

"I don't know what I would have done without you," she told him afterward. "I don't think I could have gone through with it alone."

He simply smiled. "I loved him too, you know."

This devastating and shattering event was followed by two

weeks of rest at the Santa Barbara ranch. The relaxed, yet rigid routine of the ranch was somewhat therapeutic in its own fashion.

For example, there was a midmorning trek to the stables to saddle up the horses, and then an ambling, two-hour ride on horseback through the cleared passages in the jack pine and scrub oak on the hillsides. Then the two of them had lunch in the patio of the adobe house, with cocktails perhaps, or maybe a glass of Perrier, or a single Margarita, or a daiquiri decanted from a pop-top can.

Ronnie was clearing brush in the afternoon, and working on the new tack room, and then he might set traps to catch the fieldmice that frequented the place at all times, and then he might chain-saw brush brought down by the spring storms.

"This form of relaxation is hard physical labor," Ronnie once told Nancy. "It's what puts the color in my cheeks."

Nancy smiled at him, hugging him.

"For me it's a magic place. I wish I could live here all the time."

"So do I," whispered Nancy with a hopeful prayer, even though she knew she might not get her wish as soon as she wanted it.

By the time the two of them returned to Washington, Nancy was almost herself again. But not really enough herself to ward off the attacks and assaults on her that were beginning again in the press.

The focus of her life was still Ronnie, as much as it had ever been. And the focus of his life was still Nancy, as it would always be.

The bond that held Ronnie and Nancy together was strengthened by the time they were able to spend in each other's presence. Even though the White House was the center of government of the most powerful nation on earth—was, in fact, the nexus of the tension, drama, and anxiety of the entire world—the private lives of Ronnie and Nancy became almost a homely duplication of the lives of millions of other Americans.

The day usually started at seven-thirty with a wake-up call

from the White House switchboard, exactly like the wake-up call at a motel or hotel. The President showered and shaved, then joined Nancy in the family dining room for a breakfast of cold cereal and fruit, sometimes with a boiled egg added, and a cup of decaffeinated coffee.

Ronnie and Nancy then read the papers together, and at about nine o'clock in the morning the President walked over to the Oval Office.

Nancy always tried to get about fifteen minutes of physical exercise each morning, but sometimes she was not able to arrange it. She knew in her own heart that she was not a very disciplined person about such things, but she tried to adhere to a sort of schedule to keep herself fit.

At five feet four inches, she now weighed 104, and it did not seem likely that she would gain much of her lost weight back. She tried to watch her calories, eating an occasional cookie, hot bread, or ice cream.

"I tell everybody if you want to be a size six or lose weight, just have your husband go into politics," she said, "because you'll worry if off. I'm a real worrier by nature, and that stops me from eating too much. I worry about Ronnie and the kids. I worry about my friends. I even worry if I haven't got something to worry about—what am I forgetting?"

While the President was pursuing his normal routine in the Oval Office—if any schedule adhered to by the President of the United States could be called "normal"—Nancy started out her day by overseeing the management of the Executive Mansion, consulting primarily with chief usher Rex Stouten, meeting with members of her own personal staff, planning her social schedule, and dictating all official First Lady correspondence.

As her routine gradually settled down, the First Lady found that she received about fifteen hundred letters a week, and although she did not find time to read each one herself, she received a detailed report on them from her staff. There were a lot of requests for recipes. These usually involved one of two specialties: one the President's favorite food, Nancy's version of macaroni and cheese, and the other the Reagans' version of crabmeat casserole.

There were also a number of personal comments from individuals about the White House Restoration that was being done—most of them simply friendly suggestions as to how she should go about it or complimenting her on what she was doing. Nancy also had her household bills to pay. In addition to all this, she also found time to write personal notes to close friends, each of which she signed herself.

At noon, if there were no official calls to be made, Ronnie and Nancy tried to have lunch together. Usually Nancy ate either with White House guests and the President, or alone at her desk in her upstairs office. Such a meal might consist of a salad and possibly a cup of soup.

If she had friends in, she invited them to join her at four o'clock for tea, which meant White House pastries and cookies served with either tea or coffee.

Somewhere between five-thirty and six-thirty, Ronnie returned from the office to change to his exercise clothes in the living quarters, and then went to the exercise room for twenty minutes of calisthenics and weight-lifting. During this period, Ronnie and Nancy usually talked together, discussing the day's events and details of upcoming affairs.

The primary order of Nancy's routine was dictated by one consideration only:

"My husband doesn't like to come home and not find me there. He doesn't like that at all. It's important to have someone there to talk to and to bounce your day off. You've stored up all those things and thought, 'I can't wait to tell her that!' It's an atmosphere of being together that's probably more important than anything else."

At about seven o'clock the two usually sat down to dinner. The menu was always simple and light: Yankee pot roast with lettuce salad, or broiled swordfish with green beans, lettuce, and grapefruit, or other combinations just as simple and wholesome—including Ronnie's macaroni and cheese.

It became a habit—if circumstances made it possible—for

the Reagans to eat off trays and to take a look at television during these comfortable and relaxing moments together.

"We try to watch the evening news before dinner," said Nancy. "It's about the only time we have to watch television during the work week. In fact, my idea of a wonderful, relaxing evening is to sit together watching TV or a movie we want to see."

After dinner, Ronnie usually went back to his own study, decorated by Nancy with red carpeting and a collection of western paintings on the walls. There he sat in a large easy chair and put his feet up to go over the briefing papers that had accumulated on his desk during the day.

"My husband is never really free of paperwork," Nancy noted. "He usually works until he retires. I use that time to catch up on correspondence or to review reports on proposed schedules and guest lists."

When Ronnie and Nancy had guests in—particularly in the period when Ronnie began to feel like himself again after his recuperation was complete—they sometimes served dinner and topped it off with the private screening of a motion picture they wanted to see in the White House theater. At times actors from the old days might appear on the guest list—as did James Cagney and Pat O'Brien, Ronnie's friends from the thirties who had played roles in *Ragtime,* which the Reagans showed in the screening room. Both the director, Milos Forman, and the producer, Dino De Laurentiis, were invited guests that evening.

As Ronnie's recovery continued, the social life of the Reagans became more and more central to the life-style of the White House. Ronnie and Nancy were never confirmed cardplayers, and so most of the gatherings tended to be evenings of talk or watching movies.

But the Reagan life-style continued to demand an occasional break and the opportunity to reenergize in isolation and quiet. There were now only two homes away from home that the Reagans could use. And those two homes did not include Nancy's favorite house—the house on San Onofre Drive.

And indeed the house was sold in 1982, breaking what was almost an umbilical cord joining the Reagans and the West Coast. Of course the ranch was still there—yet it was always a secondary residence, a kind of place to retreat to for temporary respite, and not a place to settle down in retirement.

But the sale of the Pacific Palisades house left two places where the Reagans could rest—Camp David, which had been a presidential hideaway ever since the days of FDR, who called it Shangri-La (it was finally renamed Camp David by President Eisenhower after his grandson), and Rancho del Cielo in Santa Barbara, California.

The advantage of Camp David was its easy accessibility. There Ronnie and Nancy could stroll in the woods, use the outdoor swimming pool in good weather, and ride horseback just as they did at their Santa Barbara retreat. There the First Couple could walk hand in hand or arm in arm free from the presence of strangers and observed only by the Secret Service agents, who became quite accustomed to this loving couple's obvious preference for each other over any others.

Meanwhile, in the primary residence, the job of redecorating the White House was proceeding under the supervision of Ted Graber—the man who had decorated the Pacific Palisades house for Nancy.

Originally, Washington had been agog with worry over the possibility that the White House would turn into a kind of High Sierras motel-modern showcase—with cowboy hats on the walls, serapes tacked up everywhere, and silver-inlaid saddles hanging about. Nothing like this happened at all. Graber was a specialist in Establishment elegance, an understated and neutral look that resembled an antique Aubusson.

He did borrow some of the nuances he had achieved in the Pacific Palisades renovation. He had used a soothing neutral color he described as "greige—a warm gray," and had upholstered cushy sofas and chairs with a red-yellow floral print to feature Nancy's favorite eighteenth-century English furniture and her Chinese porcelains.

Some of these he transplanted physically from one site to the other. The effect was pleasant and comfortable, in no way obstreperous or offensive. Graber was an adherent of "trend-resistant traditional," in the words of one observer, and displayed his particular decorating talents at their best in his work on the White House.

Graber modestly pointed out that it was Nancy who had led him all the way. "She knows what she wants, and, believe me, that's the best."

Once the comfort of the living quarters was established and publicized, the furor about Nancy's redecorating policies died down entirely.

Nancy's natural ability to love had always extended beyond her own husband and family to children whose lives had inadvertently blocked them from the love of others. During her early days in Sacramento, she had become interested in the Foster Grandparent Program, which was devoted to bringing older persons into contact with children who needed their love and affection—and care—because of special emotional problems. In the White House, she continued to sponsor the program, to urge its expansion throughout the nation, and to extend it to teenagers.

In 1981 she signed a contract with the Bobbs-Merrill Company for a book titled *To Love a Child* to be published in the fall of 1982. The book consisted of twelve accounts of relationships between foster grandparents and grandchildren who took part in the program. Nancy was to provide the introduction to the book and headnotes to the individual sections.

In addition to the book, a song titled "To Love a Child" was written and recorded by Frank Sinatra. The proceeds from the book and the recording were donated to the Foster Grandparent Program.

Nancy had also become involved in fighting drug abuse among young people. In 1981 she visited two drug rehabilitation centers—Phoenix House in New York City and Second Genesis in Upper Marlboro, Maryland—and addressed a meeting at the White House of the National Federation of Parents for Drug Free Youth.

In February 1982 she toured several drug prevention and treatment facilities in Florida and Texas to talk with teenagers and others participating in the programs. Later that month she discussed private funding and other aspects of anti-drug-abuse efforts at a luncheon she gave for governors' wives during the annual meeting in Washington of the National Governors Association. She also took part in the White House Conference on Drug Use and Families held in March 1982.

The life-style of the Reagans continued to fascinate the members of the media. Once when Ronnie and Nancy were being interviewed together in their rooms, a magazine writer asked them some questions about whether or not they "economized" in the White House.

Nancy had an answer for that one immediately. "You bet. You just don't buy as much. I mean, how else do you economize? In clothes, food—every area—we've never been extravagant people in any way, no matter what 'they' say."

Ronnie broke in: "It's been a long time since either of us bought a luxurious gift for the other on Christmas—and it sometimes bothers me. A couple of years ago our gift to each other was a hydraulic log-splitter for use at the ranch."

Nancy broke in quickly: "Every girl wants one of those."

"Last year redoing the living room at home was our Christmas present," Ronnie went on. "The way the bill came in it was worth both our birthday *and* anniversary gifts for that year."

To make up for it, Nancy determined that Christmas 1982 would be one that Ronnie would never forget. The weather cooperated with her from the first. They had opted to spend their holiday season in the White House, and the first snow of winter—six inches of it—drifted down, blanketing the White House grounds, making it look like one of those picture-postcard New England winter wonderlands.

Now Nancy went to work, fixing up the White House so that it was festooned in an old-fashioned Yuletide decor. The decorations gave the public rooms an aura Nancy thought of as truly "magical." The chandeliers, brass, and marble all glistened. Huge green wreaths hung in the windows, dotted with red berries. There were boughs of holly and hundreds of red and white poinsettias placed about. There were white roses mixed with boxwood and magnolia leaves—the whole nestled in bowls placed in the three first-floor parlors—sending a spicy aroma up into the air.

In the East Room, Nancy had gathered a collection of small Christmas trees, decorated with flickering firefly-like lights.

In the Blue Room, the center piece was an eighteen-and-a-half-foot Fraser fir from North Carolina bedecked with silver and gold metallic snowflakes made at the First Lady's request by a drug-rehabilitation group in the Washington area. Adorning that tree—and two smaller ones in niches nearby—were almost a hundred pounds of California walnuts wrapped in lace.

The White House social calendar was crowded with holiday events. There was a ball for members of Congress, a party for children of foreign diplomats, receptions for the Secret Service, the White House staff members, and the press.

Ronnie and Nancy spent Christmas Day at the White House with twenty close friends and members of the family before they headed west for Palm Springs, where they would celebrate New Year's Day.

The Christmas board groaned with traditional Yuletide fare: roast turkey with chestnut dressing, giblet gravy, mashed potatoes, carrots in turnip cups, and chocolate Yule logs accompanied by California table wines.

The New Year was spent at the huge Xanadu-like estate of the Walter Annenbergs near Palm Springs—with its twelve lakes on 250 acres, a golf course, and the Mayanesque main house sprawled out over 32,600 square feet, furnished with the best in contemporary furniture and hung with original oils by Van Gogh, Gauguin, Rodin, and others. Leonore Annenberg served at that time as the White House chief of protocol.

After Michael Reagan's enthusiastic support for his father in the 1980 campaign—he delivered six hundred speeches in thirty-five states for the Reagan-Bush cause—the older Reagan son got back into the powerboat-racing business in 1982 by founding a marine marketing company in Los Angeles. Calling it M.C.R.—Michael Colleen Reagan (Colleen was his wife's name)—he sold powerboats, and did so quite successfully, as it developed.

Later in the year, Larry Smith, the head of a speedboat-racing team, approached Michael and invited him to pilot a powerboat up the Mississippi River. Michael agreed to do so, but only if Smith would use the promotion scheme to raise money for the United States Olympic Committee.

The idea was to invite individual donors and corporate sponsors to pledge donations for the upcoming games in Los Angeles on the basis of each mile completed in the "race" up the river from New Orleans to St. Louis. In return for the money put up, each sponsor would have a decal of the company name painted on the boat and would thus be featured whenever the boat was seen or photographed.

In August 1982 the race began, with Michael at the helm of Larry Smith's thirty-eight-foot *Scarab* racer. Michael succeeded in setting a record in a somewhat spectacular twenty-five-hour-and-eleven-minute rush up the river. In all, the *Scarab* racing team raised $500,000 for the United States Olympic Committee.

Ronnie flew in from Washington to attend a dinner in honor of Michael after the finish of the race. It was a festive father-and-son occasion.

In April 1983, on the twelfth, Michael became the father of a little girl—Ashley Marie Reagan. This was the President's second grandchild—another cause for celebration in the White House.

And, as if that weren't excitement enough, Michael was again approached by Larry Smith to make another power-boat race—this time from Chicago to Detroit through the Great Lakes.

Michael managed to attain clips of eighty-five miles per hour, making the entire trip in twelve hours, thirty-four minutes, and forty-one seconds—a benchmark record.

What came to be called the "Assault on the Great Lakes" raised a total of $250,000, once again for the United States Olympic Committee, by means of the sponsorship pledges

To newsmen, Michael related a fantasy he lived in some of his daydreams. In the fantasy, the President is seated in Chasen's restaurant in Beverly Hills—his old hangout from his early motion-picture days—when some tourists enter.

"Who is that?" one of them asks.

"That's Michael Reagan's father," explains Chasen.

As for his younger sister, Patti, she had done her best to distance herself from her parents when Ronald Reagan was Governor of California by changing her professional acting name from Reagan to Davis. And, for a time, that had proved sufficient to keep off the press.

But when her father was elected to the White House, Patti found herself totally opposed to the notion that she was the daughter of the President of the United States.

"I dreaded his getting elected. I said I couldn't handle that—and I wasn't really able to."

Trying to do what was right by her mother and father, she let herself be measured for a Dior original to wear to the 1981 inauguration, though she still was more comfortable in sweatsuits and jeans.

The inauguration itself was an exhausting affair for Patti.

"I didn't have very much success walking in that dress. I think I ripped it in about three places. As I remember, I had masking tape on the hem by the end of the evening. I sort of walk like a baseball player. Not exactly grace in motion."

It was the aftermath of the inauguration that caused her the most grief. Back in Santa Monica she found herself quite definitely ill.

"I got really sick. I couldn't breathe and had to be taken to the hospital emergency ward."

They told her she was suffering from emotional stress. It was as if her body had gone into shock. She was treated and returned home, where she went through a week of bed rest.

Although her parents were concerned over her health, they

left her alone so as not to aggravate the situation. Patti finally understood that she had simply experienced a near nervous collapse after the emotional exhaustion caused by the excitement of the inauguration.

As she recuperated, she began to see herself in a slightly different light. She realized that things would happen in her life that she might find difficult to cope with. She determined to handle such adversities in the future and try to mature a bit as a person.

Her parents saw her during her recuperation—but always on the Coast, not in Washington. Not going to Washington was Patti's own choice.

"That stuff about not being asked to the White House is *ridiculous!* I can go there anytime I want—but it's not my world. I enjoy seeing [my parents] more in California on the ranch. It's more private."

Rumors of estrangement between her and her mother reached her ears during her recuperation.

"This is just a pack of lies. I wish the press would stop picking on my mother. She has very independent children. My parents are tolerant and accepting of us."

In the summer of 1983, Patti Davis made her stage debut in a summer-stock production of *Vanities* at the Cherry County Playhouse in Traverse City, Michigan.

During the show's preview, Ronnie and Nancy sent a good-luck telegram from the White House to their youngest daughter.

"They might have come if the show were going to run longer than two weeks," Patti said. "But they are sensitive about upstaging either my brother Ronnie or me. If they came, it would become *their* show."

She did well in her stage debut and returned to California with another honor to her credit.

It was now the middle of Ronald Reagan's first Administration, and Nancy had almost completely shaken off her assassination malaise. She never gained back her weight, but she gained back her confidence and she gained back her cool. This was largely accomplished by the fact that criticism of the Reagan Administration pretty well died down when the recession began to fade and Nancy's style of living did not any longer seem so outrageous to the media.

She changed her demeanor a bit, too, deliberately altering the way she gazed at her husband in public. The worshipful stare that had antagonized so many people vanished. She found also that she could go it alone without hunkering down and hiding from the public.

She even learned to joke with the press—a new tack for her, but one she took to easily. The results softened her media image. For example, on one visit to a school in the South, one of the boys asked her how she liked being married to the President.

"Fine," Nancy told him with a bright smile, "as long as the President is Ronald Reagan."

Score one for the First Lady's light touch!

A little girl asked her if she got tired of all the traveling around in her job.

"There's an old saying," Nancy told her. "You play the cards that are dealt you. You just do it."

Ronnie and Nancy remained unapologetic lovers throughout their White House years, with their unalloyed affection evident to the public and to the press at all times, no matter who was present. On occasion, it could be upsetting to some watchers, who misunderstood and thought the two of them were putting on an act of some kind left over from the Golden Years of Hollywood.

But romance never deserted the Reagan relationship. Ronnie continued his yearly habit of ordering a bouquet of flowers from a special Hollywood shop to be delivered to Edith Davis, Nancy's mother, on Nancy's birthday. On the note, Ronnie always wrote the same thing:

"Thanks for giving me Nancy."

Secret Service agents and others close to the Reagans became quite used to seeing the two long-married lovers sitting on a sofa in the dark at Camp David, watching a motion picture and holding hands and eating popcorn out of a shared bowl.

"It's like looking at a pair of high school kids," one aide commented.

And Nancy continued to observe the amenities when it came to birthdays and anniversaries. Even though Ronnie knew he had a birthday coming, and even though he knew Nancy would remember it, she always managed to surprise him in some fashion—making it a little more memorable than just an ordinary daily event.

In 1983, for example, the President was in the midst of a televised press conference in the White House on February 4, dealing with all sorts of probing questions and important international considerations. In the middle of the questions, Nancy appeared out of nowhere, carrying a birthday cake on a platter, with one lighted candle flickering in the middle of the frosting! The President would be seventy-two two days later, on February 6.

Everybody sang "Happy Birthday" to Ronnie that day—on national television.

During Christmas 1983, Nancy and Ronnie's daughter, Patti, brought Paul Grilley to the White House to meet the President and the First Lady. Grilley was a teacher of yoga, studying for a Bachelor of Science degree in kinesiology at UCLA. He was the son of a carpenter and a secretary in Glacier Park, Montana.

Both he and Patti were vegetarians, nonsmokers, and teetotalers, except for a little white wine at mealtimes. Grilley taught at the Yoga College of India in Beverly Hills.

In April 1984, the two of them traveled to Paris to work on a fashion layout for Michael Jacobs. It was in Paris that Grilley proposed to Patti, and bought her a ring of gold and mother-of-pearl. Patti immediately telephoned to her mother in Washington, and the news went out that the two were engaged. No date was set at that time for the wedding, however.

Two months earlier, in February, Patti's brother Ron resigned from the Joffrey II ballet to become a free-lance journalist. One of his first stories was an article for *Newsweek* telling why he had decided to quit.

In the article, published in the February 14 issue of the magazine, he wrote:

"I left because I want to make a home with my wife and to one day have a child. The finances of ballet and the prospect of touring for months on end made these goals distantly attainable at best. . . . I admit my mistake [in becoming a dancer]: ballet is much more and much less than I'd imagined as an eighteen-year-old."

He was making $90 a week as a ballet dancer, and $270 a week when he was on tour. He felt that this did not add up to enough to support a family. His article pointed out that the ballet world should pay its dancers on a more equable basis in order to get top talent—and keep it.

Meanwhile, Nancy and Ronnie were beginning to step up their social pace a bit. Once the President was out of the woods after his operation, it was decided that his traveling schedule should be increased. There were several round-the-world trips—or at least the combined itinerary added up to a trip around the world.

In the summer of 1982, for example, the Reagans had traveled to Ireland, England, France, Germany, and Italy. Hand in hand, the two of them strolled about like ordinary sightseers— perhaps a bit more affectionate than the average husband and wife—and saw lands they had heard about and read about years before.

In France, they visited the site of the Normandy invasion landings on D-Day some thirty-seven years before, and Nancy looked at the cliffs the soldiers of World War II had to climb, and wondered how in the world any of them ever got up them.

"The grayness, the drizzle," she recalled later, "everything tended to make it very emotional."

In Rome they visited Pope John Paul II for a short interview. As they left the Vatican they were surrounded by a group of visiting Americans—all of them priests—who sang "God Bless America" to them as they held hands with the Pope smiling on. It brought tears to Nancy's eyes, and also to Ronnie's.

In England, Ronnie rode horseback with the Queen of England and then had a ride through Windsor Home Park with Prince Philip.

But the most memorable trip occurred almost two years later in 1984 when they decided to visit the Orient. It was an affair of state, trying to keep ajar the doors that had been first opened by President Richard M. Nixon some years before.

It was, of course, an election year, and the press was more interested in who was going to run against Ronald Reagan than in Ronald Reagan himself. In order to forestall the age factor that everyone knew would be a part of the coming campaign, Ronnie went out of his way to show himself as fit as a fiddle during a special two-day stopover in Hawaii.

With Nancy looking on, Ronnie came charging down onto the beach at Waikiki with his swim trunks on, took a brief dip in the warm waters off the shore, and splashed about for the cameras that were watching nearby. There was even time for clowning around, and Nancy watched as a playful aide of the President tossed him a coconut, miming a forward pass, with Ronnie catching it handily and performing a halfback swivel along the high-tide line.

The highlight of that trip occurred in Peking, the seat of the Chinese government, where they visited Xian, where the two-thousand-year-old tomb of the first Emperor of China was located. They stood arm in arm in front of a large terra-cotta group statue done in a kind of bas-relief, depicting an ancient Chinese army that seemed to be riding out of the distance toward them.

And in Peking they slept in an imposing replica of a Ming Dynasty dragon bed with a pillared canopy stretched over it. After being wined and dined by the Chinese, the American visitors threw a huge spread for six hundred guests at the Great Wall Hotel—serving American tom turkey, seafood mousse, and praline ice cream. There was also California red wine, white wine, and champagne.

There was no end of excitement. The Chinese police received a bomb threat, presumably against the Great Wall Hotel when the Reagans were staying there, but no bombing happened.

"Neighbors are not family," Ronnie said at one point during the visit, "but they can be dear and trusted friends." It was his way of saying that he actually *liked* the country and the Chinese people—and he believed that they liked him as well.

Ronnie and Nancy were inseparable throughout the trip. She had developed an anti-jet-lag diet that Ronnie adhered to during the trip so that he would not be too bushed during the first days to enjoy the sights. There were three days of sightseeing around China's Great Wall, too, and several days in bustling Shanghai.

Much more time was spent at home than on the road, and it was at home that Ronnie and Nancy showed the depth of their commitment to each other. The influence of one upon the other became even stronger during those years. Although no one had ever suggested that Ronald Reagan was not his own man—no one, that is, aside from critics on the other side of the political fence who made such claims as a matter of course—Nancy established herself more firmly as a factor in her husband's actions.

For example, there was the time Soviet Foreign Minister Andrei Gromyko was in the Reagan quarters at the White House after a diplomatic meeting in Washington. Nancy was on hand to make the visitor from Moscow feel at home during natural breaks in the long official conversations.

Over a glass of fruit juice for Gromyko and a Perrier for the First Lady, Nancy began to charm the diplomat.

Quite abruptly Gromyko dropped the small talk and assumed the mantle of Russian gloom. "Does your husband believe in peace or war?" he asked Nancy with the obvious expectation of an evasive answer.

Nancy never hesitated. "Peace."

"You're sure?" More Russian gloom.

Nancy was sure, and she told Gromyko so. The conversation then veered back into the genteel and superficial channels in which it had at first lightly sailed. When he was ready to join the President again, Gromyko went back to the central point.

"Well, then," he told Nancy, "you whisper *peace* in his ear every night."

Nancy nodded with a smile, not to be put off by the Russian's sophisticated onslaught. "I will," she promised. "I'll whisper it in *your* ear."

She had grown in those White House years—and the love affair between Ronnie and Nancy had also grown in the same proportion into something rich and powerful.

Their obvious love for each other was never allowed to remain beneath the surface for long. It was partly due to their individual personalities. Ronnie had never lost that gee-whiz appeal that had been part of his image for decades.

"When something unusual happens," he once confessed to Nancy, "or something important in my life, or something that I hear about, the first thing in my mind is, 'Wait till I tell you!' It's that way between the two of us."

They shared decisions, too—especially crucial ones. When it came time for the all-important choice to be made between running for reelection and "choosing" not to run, Ronnie was of two minds. He was aware how deeply the assassination attempt had affected Nancy.

He began approaching her in a manner that indicated to her that he *did* want to try. Although she shuddererd at the thought of it, as he knew she would, she began to reconsider her original desire not to run, knowing that if he *really* wanted the presidency again, it would be wrong to refuse.

"I like the presidency," he told her. "I like what I'm doing. But it's not the last thing in the world."

"But you've done it already for three and a half years."

"I think it may take another four years to really turn everything around."

"The country's already better off now, thanks to you!" Nancy protested.

"But it could be even *better* off. I want to make sure I've really turned it around before I leave Washington."

There were more conversations, and eventually the decision was made to try again—even though every fiber of Nancy's being intuitively said: "Stop!"

When she looked back on those conversations, she realized how subtly and how completely Ronnie had been able to sway her from her own way of thinking to his way of thinking.

"I guess he was wooing me," she confessed ruefully.

And of course she did agree to the effort.

The run for reelection was a rerun of the 1980 campaign. Now Nancy knew what to do, and she did everything assigned to her in a superlative fashion. She had learned a great deal about electioneering and winning friends and influencing people during the first campaign. She had learned how to play the First Lady the way she should play the role—as a serene and smiling public presence. She perfected the role, added important little nuances as the campaign progressed, and wound up costarring with the winner.

"You're as good an instinctive politician as Ronnie is," one aide complimented her in 1984. "You're more tactical, he's more strategic. A good campaign needs both. One without the other won't work."

It may have tired her out and exhausted her in the day-to-day grind, but she maintained her poise throughout the grueling days and nights—and somehow she managed to get through it.

"Well," she remarked once, "it *is* a job, which I didn't quite realize before."

During the nomination proceedings in Dallas, the romantic relationship that the President and First Lady still enjoyed— and had enjoyed through thick and thin in all their years together—surfaced briefly and dramatically during Nancy's appearance before the convention prior to the nominee's arrival to accept the party's nomination.

As Nancy stood at the microphone, making a short statement of thanks and appreciation, there was a simultaneous picture of Ronnie as he sat in the hotel suite watching the proceedings projected on a huge television screen mounted behind her.

She turned to look at him, at his huge replica projected on the screen, and raised both arms and called out his name. The President finally looked down at her and waved with a big smile on his face—the two of them, separated by space only, together electronically and spiritually in an unforgettable picture.

It was a memorable moment—a symbolic representation of their eternal and inseparable attachment to one another.

There was more togetherness in evidence in Dallas than simply that of Ronnie and Nancy. Their youngest son, Ron, was making his debut as a columnist in that very city, writing up the Republican National Convention for the *Dallas Morning News*. It was fitting that he chose to write his initial column about Ronald Reagan's family.

Ideally, Ron wrote, a candidate and his family should appear to the nation to be "as accessible as Disneyland and just as harmless."

However, he went on to say, it was not quite that simple at all. "The irony is that we are normal people," he said of himself, his sisters, Maureen and Patti, and his older brother, Michael.

While Maureen disagreed with the President on the proposed Equal Rights Amendment to the Constitution and Patti had her own views on nuclear disarmament, such differences usually did not extend far enough for any of the children to withdraw support from their father.

The column was Ron's first appearance in any newspaper after his retirement from the Joffrey II ballet and from dancing in general.

Patti also proved to be virtually inseparable from her mother and father and brother. Since the announcement of her engagement, Nancy had spent a great deal of time with her daughter planning for the upcoming wedding, which was finally scheduled for the middle of August.

Patti had changed in some ways, and now chose to be married in a traditional ceremony. She and Paul Grilley decided to exchange plain gold wedding bands during the ceremony, scheduled to be held in the garden of the Hotel Bel-Air, where Patti used to attend dancing classes when she lived in Pacific Palisades.

The ceremony was private, including a little over a hundred family members and friends. It was the President himself who escorted his daughter down the aisle and, when asked by the Reverend Donn Moomaw of the Bel-Air Presbyterian Church who was giving away the bride, the President responded: "Her mother and I do."

The bride wore a bracelet originally belonging to her great-grandmother on Nancy's side of the family (something old), a long off-the-shoulder gown of white silk lace and charmeuse, with a slight train and veil (something new), a ring lent her by a friend (something borrowed), and a garter (something blue).

One of Patti's attendants was her sister-in-law, Doria Reagan, Ron's wife. Also present were Anne Allman, the Reagans' longtime housekeeper, and Barney Barnett, Ronnie's driver when he had served as Governor of California.

Once the wedding was over, Ronnie and Nancy returned to the more onerous obligations of the election campaign. And it proceeded almost without a hitch. The hitch that surfaced was the slump Ronald Reagan experienced in the public polls during the campaign when he appeared to be overstuffed with facts and unable to express himself in his usual precise style at the first debate.

Nancy was beside herself with distress after the debate was over. She immediately sought out his aides.

"What did you do to my husband?"

But it seemed fairly obvious that Ronnie was simply bloated with excess data.

And so the two of them sat down together and Nancy told her husband to be himself and to answer the questions simply and clearly.

She knew, of course, that it was more easily said than done.

Certainly Ronnie had to master the facts necessary for the debate and certainly he had to be able to come up with suitable answers to the questions.

But it was his uncharacteristic nervousness that bothered Nancy. And she devised a plan to try to break up that nervousness. She did it by using Ronnie's own tactics—or what she presumed might be his tactics.

Midway in the second rehearsal—each candidate selected devil's advocates among his aides to act as the press representatives and the opposition—Ronnie was struggling with a particularly difficult question that had him frowning, and scratching his head, and looking uncomfortable, when suddenly—

There stood Nancy right in the middle of the floor, dressed in slacks and a Windbreaker. As Ronnie glanced up with a frown of annoyance, she unzipped the Windbreaker and held it wide at her sides. Ronnie read the huge words that lettered a V-necked sweater underneath:

4 MORE IN '84

The President broke up, howling with laughter. The tension was broken. Nancy retreated, knowing that what she had hoped would happen had indeed happened.

Whether it was what Nancy did or simply that Ronnie was ready for the fight the second time, the President scored heavily in the second debate—even vanquishing the one inevitable "factor" that the opposition hoped would help them: the age factor.

From that moment on, there was no looking back. The Reagan ticket won forty-nine of the fifty states for a smashing triumph, losing only Minnesota and Washington, D.C.

Only one thing marred the President's tremendous victory. In the early morning hours of Monday, the day preceding the election, Nancy rose from bed in the Reagan suite at the Red Lion Inn in Sacramento, failed to recall that the bed was mounted on a platform, and missed her step to fall on the floor and strike her head on a chair near the bed.

The next day, the wrap-up of the campaign, was a busy one, and she attended three rallies with Ronnie—showing some signs of fatigue and difficulty in maintaining her balance.

On election day she was still experiencing periods of dizziness, and when the helicopter carrying her and her husband landed at Santa Monica, California, Nancy slipped a bit on the step and had to catch herself on the handrail.

Ronnie was beside himself with concern, and almost called off the victory celebration following the election results, but she talked him out of it. Her headaches, which were suspected at one point to be caused by a possible concussion, vanished in a few days, and there were no recurrences.

But now, when everything was relaxed and calm, Nancy made an uncharacteristic gaffe. Her usual manner was not to say anything, and to let the media define what she meant by her laconic comments. Now suddenly she told the *Washington Times* that yes, she had always been a little anemic—nearly all her life.

And then she said that her husband and her stepson, Michael, were "estranged." "There is an estrangement and has been for three years," she said. "And I really think we should now say this and get it all done with so we can put these questions behind us.

"There is an estrangement. We are sorry about it. We hope that someday it will be solved. We do not believe and have never believed in discussing family problems in public."

Well!

Sure enough, at the ranch that Thanksgiving, Michael was not there. But that did not deter the press from locating him. Sure enough, Michael had something to say about that "estrangement." If there was any dispute, Michael told the media, it stemmed from Nancy's "jealousy."

"We have the only two grandchildren of the President," Michael said, referring of course to Cameron Michael Reagan and to Ashley Maria Reagan. "I have noticed . . . that Nancy has not been as warm toward us. She would like it to have her kids have the grandchildren of the President." And those "kids," of course, were Ron and Patti Reagan.

When Nancy read the newspapers, she was floored once again. "What should we do?" she asked Ronnie. Ronnie shrugged, not knowing what to do. He had always kept his hands off the children and let things take their course. But this time Nancy's anguish got to him.

He telephoned Michael, and the wires heated up. Someone hung up. There was another telephone call. Again the conversation was terminated.

The press picked up the conflict. Newspaper stories mentioned "facts" about Michael's first marriage—the one that had broken up after ten months. Michael blamed the First Lady on these "whispers" that appeared in the press.

It was, he told reporters, "unfair." "I can't believe this is the First Lady of our country doing this. If she is doing this to me, what is she going to do to the people?"

He suggested in part that perhaps the "bump on the head" his stepmother had received on the day before the election had prompted her to talk of a family estrangement.

Now the President called Michael again, fuming. Michael hung up. But he appeared before the press again, this time wearing a T-shirt with these bold letters printed on it:

I'M NOT THE DANCER.

He also made some remarks about his sister Maureen's first two marriages and her manner of lecturing audiences.

This brought Maureen into the fray. She complained immediately that her brother had a "vendetta" going against Nancy; she said that it left the First Lady and the President "just agonized." She accused him of "making these flip remarks he thinks are funny but hurt people"—particularly the words on his T-shirt and his remarks about Maureen's marriages.

"I think Michael should seek professional help," she said.

With the escalation of an inconsequential remark into a fam-

ily brawl, Nancy and Ronnie were once again beside themselves with grief. Things had been said that never should have
been said. And yet the truth was that they simply did not like
to air their family problems in public. It was not their way.

Quietly and circumspectly, Ronnie and Nancy set about
making things neat again. Michael and his family were invited
to the White House for Christmas. It was there that the President and his grandson, Cameron, built a big snowman on the
front lawn of the White House.

However, when it was all over, and the photographers were
assembled to take a picture of it, they discovered that there was
a tiny replica of the big snowman to one side. And it was there
that Cameron was standing, proudly showing it off.

"Grandfather made the big one," Cameron told the press.
"This one is mine."

By January, after a three-hour visit between father, stepmother, and son in a Los Angeles hotel suite, Nancy was able
to declare to the press:

"All is resolved. Everybody loves each other."

But of course, they always did anyway.

Meanwhile, for her work in helping elect her father President for the second time, Maureen was presented by Nancy
with a tiny doll dressed up as a cheerleader. It was Nancy's
way of extending her personal thanks to her stepdaughter for a
job well done.

As the date of the inauguration approached, the Reagans became the relaxed lovers they had always been. Nancy even admitted that there was a tremendous elation and excitement to
the second inauguration—"like when you get married"—even
though she had at first "dragged [her] heels" against the run
for the presidency.

She told a *Good Morning America* audience on ABC-TV
that she was "so excited that I don't remember everything"
that happened when the President was sworn in for the first
time in 1981. As for whether the second inauguration was a
comedown from the first, she said flatly:

"Oh, I don't feel that way. I find that moments that are very,

very exciting and emotional . . . I can barely remember [in detail]. I was so excited that I don't remember everything at the first inaugural. Now this time I'll remember . . . I hope."

The inauguration itself was spoiled only by the weather—something that could certainly be overlooked even though it did put a damper (psychologically *and* physically) on the proceedings.

There were two swearing-in ceremonies. The first—the official one—was held in the White House Grand Foyer, at the foot of the forty-step marble staircase that links the upstairs family quarters with the rooms of state.

Chief Justice Warren E. Burger administered the constitutionally prescribed thirty-five-word oath, with Nancy, wearing a wool dress of her own special "Reagan red," holding the family Bible that belonged to Ronnie's mother, Nelle.

When it was all over, Burger said, "Congratulations," to the President.

Ronnie turned to Nancy. "I'm going to kiss you now," he said. And he did, adding an affectionate hug as well.

Then the Reverend Donn Moomaw, the pastor of the Bel-Air Presbyterian Church, which Ronnie and Nancy had attended when they lived in Los Angeles, delivered the invocation, praying that the oath-taking would be "more than a formality" and would instead be "a splendid new time of commitment and dedication."

Prescott Bush, brother of Vice-President George Bush, attended the ceremonies and was struck in particular by the obvious affectionate relationship enjoyed by the President and the First Lady.

"As she stood holding the Bible while her husband took his oath of office," he wrote in a reminiscence, "the love that shone in her eyes as she watched him lit up the whole area around them."

And so it did, as it always seemed to do wherever the two of them went together.

March that year came in like a lamb, after one of the most ferocious and devastating winters on record. On the fourth,

Ronnie and Nancy had been married for thirty-three years. Because of upcoming talks with the Russians and the imminent arrival of certain diplomats and world leaders in Washington, the President and First Lady were unable to celebrate their anniversary alone together at the Santa Barbara ranch.

Instead, at noon the doors of the Oval Office closed on the two of them, allowing them to enjoy a quiet luncheon together. When they reappeared later and were asked by eager members of the press what had transpired at their wedding anniversary, both smiled but did not enlighten anyone as to what they had talked about.

There was the revelation of a gift, however.

"We gave each other a pickup truck for the ranch," the President said, with what could be described as the ghost of a twinkle in his eye.

The First Lady herself appeared secretly amused. Was she thinking of what she had once said about a similar gift for the ranch—"Every girl wants one of those"?

In a way, the gift itself seemed to symbolize the practicality, the durability, and the indestructibility of the American Dream—the dream that Ronald Reagan had revitalized during his first term of office and that in large part depended for its revitalization on the hope, the faith, and—above all—the love these two people shared.

In the familiar words used by ancient storytellers to close out a classic love story—

And they lived happily ever after.